MUSIC FROM
TAIZÉ

VOLUME I
Conceived and edited by Brother Robert
Composed by Jacques Berthier

VOCAL EDITION

COLLINS

MUSIC FROM TAIZÉ — VOLUME I
is available in three editions

Vocal edition   ISBN 0 00 599720 8
Instrumental edition   ISBN 0 00 599721 6
People's edition   ISBN 0 00 599952 9

Also available
MUSIC FROM TAIZÉ — VOLUME II

Vocal edition   ISBN 0 00 599863 8
Instrumental edition   ISBN 0 00 599883 2
People's edition   ISBN 0 00 599884 0

Recordings: available as records or cassettes
from Christian booksellers

CANTATE!

CANONS ET LITANIES

RESURREXIT

HarperCollins*Religious*
a division of HarperCollins*Publishers*
77–85 Fulham Palace Road
Hammersmith, London W6 8JB

Collins Dove
PO Private Bag 200, Burwood, Victoria 3125

Collins Liturgical New Zealand
PO Box 1, Auckland

First published, this edition, 1982
Ninth printing 1993

All requests for mechanical license or for reprint rights for
the material in this edition are to be addressed to
HarperCollins*Religious*

Made and Printed in Great Britain
by Bell & Bain Ltd, Glasgow

TABLE OF CONTENTS

I. OSTINATO RESPONSES AND CHORALES   (1)

II. LITANIES AND OTHER TEXTS WITH REFRAINS   (40)

III. ACCLAMATIONS   (72)

IV. CANONS   (82)

FOREWORD

THE TAIZÉ COMMUNITY

The Community

Taizé is a tiny village hidden away in the hills of Burgundy, in the eastern part of France not far from the town of Cluny. Since 1940 it has been the home of an ecumenical community of brothers whose prayer, three times each day, is at the center of their life. Today, Taizé is a place to which visitors of all ages and backgrounds come on pilgrimage, to participate in international meetings of prayer and reflection.

Brother Roger first came to the village of Taizé in 1940, at the age of twenty-five. He dreamt of starting a community "on account of Christ and the Gospel", and he chose to do so in an area, in those years, strongly marked by human distress. It was wartime, and his house became a place of welcome for refugees, especially Jews, fleeing from the Nazi occupation. After living alone for two years he was joined by his first brothers, and in 1949, when there were seven of them, they committed themselves, for life, to celibacy and to life together. Year after year, other brothers make the same monastic commitments.

At first, the community was made up of brothers from different Protestant denominations. Today it includes many Catholics as well. By its very nature Taizé is an ecumenical community. It is also international. Its eighty or so brothers come from some twenty different countries throughout the world. All the brothers do not always remain in Taizé; some live in small groups, known as fraternities, among the poor on different continents. One of these is located in a poor section of New York City. Since 1966, members of an international Catholic congregation of sisters, who live according to the spirit of St. Ignatius of Loyola, have taken responsibility for a large part of the work of welcoming people to Taizé; their house is located in a nearby village.

Taizé's vocation is to strive for communion among all. From its beginnings, the community has worked for reconciliation among Christians split apart into different denominations. But the brothers do not view reconcilation among Christians as the end in itself: it concerns all of humanity, since it makes the Church a place of communion for all.

Taizé and the young

During the first twenty years of its existence, the community lived in relative isolation. Then, gradually, young people between the ages of 18 and 30 began coming to Taizé, in ever-increasing numbers. Out of this grew the idea of holding a "Council of Youth". Announced in 1970, it began at Taizé in 1974 with 40,000 people present. For years it has involved people from all over the world in a common search.

In Taizé itself this search takes place during the international meetings which bring young people, from many different countries, together, throughout much of the year. Participants enter into the prayer of the community, and share their lives and concerns with one another. They look for ways of living lives of prayer and commitment in their own local situations. Others come to Taizé to confront their lives with the Gospel in the solitude of a silent retreat.

But this search is not limited only to Taizé. Through meetings and visits, it spreads out to many countries and continents. From time to time letters are written by the young people to allow others, as well, to reflect on the questions and topics which are so crucial for them.

In 1974, for example, a group of young people from every continent drafted a *First Letter to the People of God,* which called upon Christians to be, at one and at the same time, "a contemplative people, thirsting for God; a people of justice, living the struggle of the exploited; a people of communion, where the non-believer also finds a creative place." On the same occasion, Brother Roger wrote a personal letter entitled *A Life We Never Dared Hope For.*

A *Second Letter to the People of God* was written in 1976, by Brother Roger and another intercontinental group of young people at Calcutta, during a stay of several weeks there among the poorest of the poor. As a contribution to a different future for all, says the letter, "the People of God can build up a parable of sharing in the human family." The letter goes on to discuss some concrete ways of sharing, and more concrete suggestions were proposed the following year in a *Letter to All Generations,* written on the South China Sea amidst people living on junks in the water.

The *Acts of the Council of Youth 1979* were written in one of the worst slums of Africa, Kenya's Mathare Valley, where Brother Roger wrote the letter, *The Wonder of a Love.* The texts were made public during a "European meeting" which brought 15,000 people to Paris in December 1978. These *Acts* announce the end of a winter, a springtime of the Church. They make a number of concrete suggestions, urging people among other things to take an active part in the life of local Christian communities, parishes and congregations. The Council of Youth in fact has never wished to be a "movement" apart, organized around Taizé, but rather a current of communion, stimulating everyone to become more committed in their own particular situation.

1980-81: A pilgrimage across Europe and North America

To sum up four years of searching among the poor and outcast, Brother Roger and a group of young people wrote a *Letter to All Communities.* They prepared it in late 1979 while sharing the life of a poor district of Temuco, in the south of Chile. The letter is addressed both to "small provisional communities" and to "parishes and congregations, those large communities at the 'base' of the Church". It calls them to leave behind passivity, discouragement, and rivalries, to enter into a "common creation" with a "preferential option for the poor and the young". And since no one can take part in a creation with others without beginning a personal creation within themselves, the letter includes the *Itinerary for a Pilgrim,* to help everyone to set out and follow Christ. These texts were made public during a European meeting held in Barcelona.

As a concrete means of undertaking this "common creation", people both young and old have begun small pilgrimages in many different places. They are like rivulets of prayer and communion flowing into a larger river — a larger pilgrimage with stopping-points in different countries. During the year 1980, Brother Roger joined young people for gatherings of prayer in Spain, Belgium, West and East Germany, and North America. In October, prayers were held in the Roman Catholic cathedral of New York City and the Episcopal cathedral of Washington D.C.. The following month, similar gatherings took place in Montreal, Ottawa and Toronto. From 27 December 1980 to 1 January 1981, thirty thousand young people came to Rome for a European meeting. They were welcomed by 150 parishes of the city, as well as by many schools and religious communities. Prayers were held twice a day simultaneously in three basilicas: St. John Lateran, St. Mary Major and St. Mary of the Angels. A prayer was held with Pope John Paul II in St. Peter's Basilica, which proved to be too small to contain the crowds.

In 1981 the international pilgrimage continued, with stopping-points in such countries as Portugal, Great Britain, Germany, and the United States. A *Letter from Italy,* made public at the European meeting in Rome and centered on the theme of reconciliation, served as a basis for reflection in all these meetings.

For more information

— The *Letter from Taizé,* a monthly newsletter published in eight languages, including English. Subscriptions can be had by writing to Taizé.

— J. L. Gonzalez Balado, *The Story of Taizé* (Mowbray's 1980); Rex Brico, *Taizé: Brother Roger and His Community* (Collins, 1978).

— The Seabury Press (New York) and Mowbray's Publishing Co. (Oxford, London) are currently publishing the complete works of Brother Roger in English, including a new edition of The Rule of Taizé entitled *Parable of Community: Basic Texts of Taizé.*

Address: 71250 TAIZÉ-COMMUNITY, FRANCE
Telephone: (85) 50.14.14
Telex: COTAIZÉ 800753-F

MUSIC AND SONG AT TAIZÉ

In recent years, the style of singing at Taizé has greatly evolved. The first three decades saw the gradual development of a repertoire in French that answered the liturgical needs of the Community and the guests it received. Beginning with a sizeable contribution of *Chorales* and *Psalms* which have come to us from the sixteenth century, other forms were added, among them the *psalmody* created by Joseph Gelineau, and a number of liturgical pieces for *Christmas* (the first works composed for Taizé by Jacques Berthier). The question of language appeared rather quickly, since those who came to pray with the brothers were, like the brothers themselves, from an increasingly wide range of countries.

With the growing number of young people visiting Taizé since the start of the seventies, another pastoral problem presented itself. It was necessary to determine what forms of song should be employed so that all could actively *participate* in the prayer of the Community, given that the time for rehearsal is necessarily very limited. A solution had to be found in using simple elements so that a crowd of people could quickly learn them. These elements, though, had to be of real musical quality so that genuine prayer could be expressed through them.

With the help of the musician Jacques Berthier, friend of Taizé, different methods were tried out, and a solution was found in the use of *repetitive structures,* namely, short musical phrases with singable melodic units that could be readily memorized by everybody. In addition to these elements, other parts could be included (cantors, choir, instruments). A tonal or modal musical language was expressly chosen to be within the reach of all.

The use of some very simple words in basic Latin to support the music and the theme of prayer was also dictated by pastoral needs. From practical experience it was the only way of solving the unavoidable problem of languages that arose at international gatherings. At first we tried to teach everybody the five or six words of a response in one of the languages represented by the participants. But very quickly it was realized that some people were being favored while others, for whom that language was 'foreign', stumbled over the pitfalls of pronunciation.

Latin is certainly not a universal tongue, but paradoxically, since it is no longer a spoken language, Latin can assert its advantage in this context. As a dead language for everyone (whatever their native tongue, culture or social milieu), Latin is a foreign element for everyone, and hence neutral. Everyone is on an equal footing with a language that does not belong to a particular group. Its pronunciation is not difficult, and the few variations due to nationality are not important.

Finally, there is no doubting the musical sound qualities of Latin syllables. In this respect, the 'invented languages' found in some contemporary compositions come to mind. In these, small speech units are chosen to produce a particular result and act as a support to the vocal sonority. At the very worst, the use of Latin could be regarded in this light! But in fact, we receive a bonus, for these sound units compose words filled with meaning, one which is easily explained and already 'translated' into music by the musician's art and sensitivity.

This 'experimentation' with Latin was carried out at Taizé only gradually and without a ready-made theoretical justification. It began with the Praetorius canon *Jubilate Deo* and then extended little by little to the compositions requested of Jacques Berthier. There have never been unfavorable reactions from the younger generations. In fact, young people who have no memories (whether good or bad) of the liturgical Latin of a former period, generally have no specific reactions towards it (be it attraction or rejection). The very few questions that have been raised on this matter have come, as is natural, from priests or lay people who have worked with good reason, since the sixties, for a liturgy that can easily be understood by all.

In the pastoral perspective at Taizé, we never considered using long, complex phrases or whole verses in Latin. Rather, what one finds is just a few words repeated by all, as the basis of the piece.

On the other hand, living languages are widely used in the verses sung by cantors whose role is to express the prayer of all those present. At Taizé it can happen that a succession of *French, German, English, Spanish* or *Italian* etc. may occur. Such a combination of languages is more likely to be found in verse-responses and in litanies.

Brother Robert

PUBLISHER'S PREFACE

Jacques Berthier, composer and organist at St. Ignatius Church, Paris, one of the European centers of liturgical renewal, already contributed to the Taizé repertoire in the fifties. Since 1975 he has been engaged in developing a new repertoire in close collaboration with Brother Robert, one of the members of the first Taizé generation to whom the Prior, Brother Roger, confided the task of leading the music for the young people.

All the pieces in this collection have been published by Les Presses de Taizé in four successive booklets: 1. Jubilate Deo (1976); 2. Chanter le Christ (1978); 3. Chanter l'Esprit (1978); 4. Laudate Dominum (1980).

This American edition, under the general title *Music from Taizé,* contains the material from the above four books and has been substantially supplemented with new contributions by Jacques Berthier, as follows:

1 — Special melodies for English verses in a good number of pieces (ostinato responses and chorales or litanies) and an English version of a canon composed upon the harmonic pattern of the *Cantate Domino.*

2 — Three pieces written expressly on English texts in a collaboration between Taizé and the World Council of Churches Conference, held in Australia (1980), on Mission and World Evangelism: *Jesus, remember me; How blessed are you;* and *For yours is the Kingdom.*

3 — Many additional parts for choir and instruments that were especially written for the large gatherings organized by Taizé in Paris, Barcelona, Rome, etc.

In this edition, a completely new format and order has been adopted, with the help of Brother Robert, who has also written new introductions and provided practical guidelines for the performance of the music.

In this present volume all vocal parts for the people, choir and soloists are given in four groupings, each corresponding to a particular musical form. Each section is arranged in alphabetical order. A special index (p. 117) is provided to help choose pieces on a given theme, for example, psalms, meditation, Eucharist, Christmas.

The keyboard (organ or piano) and guitar parts are included in the Vocal Edition and are also contained in the Instrumental Edition which also includes parts for miscellaneous string, wind and percussion instruments. These latter parts are important for the correct utilization of the pieces and help give these musical forms their specific and original style.

Robert J. Batastini
Editor
G.I.A. Publications, Inc.

PERFORMANCE NOTES

Function

The goal towards which this music is directed is *prayer,* and most especially communal prayer, whether it be in a small group, a parish, or in a large gathering of young people, etc. And this prayer may often extend into the personal prayer of the participants; people may become aware of a certain melody running through their heads, or find themselves humming a tune: an expression of joy or confidence in God that is not always fully conscious.

The *repetitive* nature of these songs is an echo of traditions deeply rooted in Christian prayer: forms such as the Jesus Prayer among the Greek Church Fathers or, in more recent times, the Rosary in the Western Church. This way of praying can promote a kind of inner unity of the person, allowing the spirit to be more open and more attentive to what is essential.

The use of these songs in common prayer implies a certain overall *style of celebration,* one in which there is a spirit of recollection and an atmosphere of silence, where the manner of the readers or celebrants is welcoming and the elements of the prayer-space are simply arranged. In such a setting, meditative song will assume its true meaning and songs of praise will express a joy which has no need to be excited artificially.

There is, of course, no difficulty in using other music in such a context, provided that it shares the same spiritual climate. On the other hand, celebrations that are quite different in their musical characteristics styles, and purposes will gain nothing from the inclusion of one of these songs from Taizé: the two styles would only be in conflict. A choice will have to be made according to the circumstances and the nature of the celebration.

Concerning the Latin responses, some may perhaps wonder why these have not been adapted into English for this edition, seeing that the specific problem at Taizé is not usually encountered in groups, communities or parishes where a single language prevails. There are two main reasons for this:

1 — Such adaptations would seriously weaken either the accentuation of the text or the musical line which accompanies it. Changes of this sort disturb the close link which binds the music to the word-sounds which inspired the music. It would be far better to compose new music for the proposed English texts. This in fact is what Jacques Berthier has done for the several new pieces in English, as well as providing special melodies for the English verses in the ostinato responses and litanies.

2 — Furthermore, experience has clearly shown that the repetitive style quickly runs the risk of making words from one of the living languages threadbare, whereas the 'neutral' nature of a word or short phrase from a traditional liturgical language (for example, the Greek *Kyrie,* the Aramaic *Maranatha* or the Latin *Gloria*) is perfectly suited to the function of a response.

Use of these songs will readily prove that they are true means of prayer.

Performance

This music has by design avoided vocal difficulties and hence *may be sung by all.* This very fact, though, demands that attention be paid to the quality of performance, even in the simplest versions. For example:

— choose the appropriate *key* or *starting-note:* do not leave this to chance. What usually happens among people less versed in musical skills is that too low a pitch is chosen;

— do not force the sound, but attend to its *quality* and production so that the pitch does not drop;

— respect the exact value of the notes and allow the musical phrases to *'sing'*. Make sure that the syllables are properly formed so that the vowels and consonants, which are an 'incarnational' element of the spiritual value of the text and music, may be fully appreciated.

The *harmonic structure* of each piece is given in the guitar chords and keyboard accompaniment. For the sake of simplicity, only the guitar and keyboard accompaniment is published in this volume. For a small group of singers the *guitar* alone is sufficient to maintain correct tempo and pitch. It should always be unobtrusive, however, using plucked chords or arpeggios to provide a steady background of sound, and strictly avoiding staccato strums or syncopated rhythms that are foreign to the style of these pieces. In parishes, the *organ*, or another keyboard instrument, will be most useful.

All the other accompaniments are published in the second volume with practical guidelines for their use. The *melodic instruments* (flute, violin or clarinet, for example) provide many opportunities for enriching and varying the form of this style of music, or for underlining the spiritual content of a theme and the development of a prayer that moves through different nuances. These additional instruments will be particularly useful in a more lengthy version of a piece, or in celebrations involving large numbers. But equally, the simple *recorder* will bring a quality of freshness to the singing of a small group.

All sorts of combinations using the different elements of each piece are therefore possible. However, it should be emphasized that by following the guidelines given at the beginning of the four sections, the vocal parts by themselves allow very attractive versions to be realized.

Brother Robert

I

OSTINATO RESPONSES AND CHORALES

In this collection, an *ostinato* describes a musical unit sung in continuous repetition by all the people. Two different forms are employed here: the first is a short musical fragment (response), while the second is a more developed phrase (chorale). Some pieces are meditative and calm in mood (for example, *Jesus, remember me),* others give expression to a joy-filled praise *(Laudate Dominum).*

In the longer formulas, the assembly need only sing the melody, leaving the harmony to a choral group or the organ. If a choir is available, the harmony should be added gradually, beginning with the bass part, followed by the inner voices (see, for example, the chorales *How blessed are you* and *Crucem tuam).*

For responses of two measures *(Beati, Pater noster* or *Veni Sancte Spiritus)*, it will be more interesting for the assembly to sing all the vocal parts with the choir, since they are all very simple. They should be sung in a quiet, interior fashion. Against this continual body of sound, the verses sung in English by the cantor may then be clearly heard.

In all these pieces it is essential that a flow of inner life animate the singing, completely avoiding mechanical or monotonous repetition. Variations in intensity are desirable, to match the variations in the prayer itself. At times it will be calmer, and at other times more urgent. A variety of soloists, too, is often desirable, moving between different vocal timbres and ranges (e.g., a soprano followed by a baritone). In the same way, a unison chorale may be varied by beginning with a soloist, then introducing the male voices, followed by the female voices (or vice versa), and finally all the voices together.

In these editions the word *refrain* is applied only to sung units that are not repeated in ostinato fashion, but instead form the conclusion sung by the assembly to a cantor's solo part. This is the case for the pieces in the second section *(Litanies).* In this first section, two of the ostinato response themes can also be used as refrains: *Mandatum novum* and *Ubi caritas* (see Special Cases).

SPECIAL CASES

Mandatum novum

This theme may best be used either as an *ostinato* response in unison to which various elements are added (choir, passages in Latin by the sopranos, instruments), or as a *refrain* for the recitative in English.

Its structure also allows it to be sung in *canon* up to four parts, though it works best in two parts where, for example, the women's voices begin and the men's voices follow at a measure's distance. In this case the canon finishes on the final *D* of the two *dicit Dominus.*

Surrexit Dominus vere I

This chorale, with its Alleluias, may be sung by itself, accompanied by the different versions of the harmonic pattern from the *Cantate Domino* series of canons. One may also use it in combination with one or another of these canons, and of course with the corresponding choral part.

Ubi caritas

As an *ostinato* response (in unison, or in two, three or four parts) there are many possibilities for varying the texture by adding the verses ⎡B⎤ or ⎡A⎤ ⎡B⎤ from the cantors, or by using the choir or instruments.

The theme may also be used as a *refrain* either for the recitative or for the special verses ⎡C⎤ with their altered harmony.

Veni Sancte Spiritus

The regular pulse of a low A on the guitar (or *pizzicato* cello) throughout this piece provides significant support. The organ can sustain a low A on the pedal, without marking any rhythm.

The ostinato response should be sung very softly. Over this continuous background, vocal verses are sung by the cantors as desired, with some space always left after the *Veni Sancte Spiritus* which concludes each verse. A few verses in other languages are added to the two series of verses in English, as a reminder of Pentecost. Each of the instrumental solos (see Instrumental Edition, pp. 29-31) should be played as a verse with its own particular character. Instrumental and vocal verses can alternate.

Beatitudes
BEATI
Happy they who dwell in God's house.

Principal Ostinato Response

Secondary Ostinato (Unison or Canon)

Accompaniments

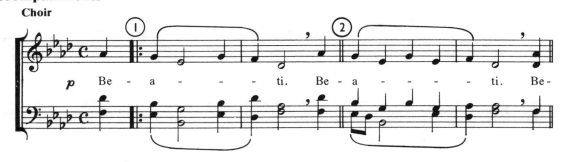

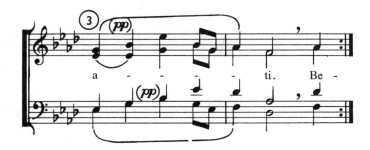

4

Keyboard

Guitar

Calmly

Verses

Cantor

1. Blest the poor in Spir - it, the King - dom of heav-en is theirs.

2. Blest are those who mourn, for they shall be com - fort - ed.

3. Blest are the low - ly, for they shall in - her - it the earth.

4. Blest are they who hun - ger and thirst for ho - li - ness, for they shall

have their fill. 5. Blest are the mer - ci - ful, for they shall ob - tain mer - cy.

6. Blest are the pure in heart, for they shall see God. 7. Blest are the

peace-mak - ers, for they shall be called the child - ren of God.

8. Blest are those per - se - cu - ted for ho - li - ness sake, for

theirs is the King-dom of heav - en.

* Choose either part.

BEATI PACIFICI

Blest are the peacemakers, and blest the pure in heart, for they shall see God.

Ostinato Chorale

Mixed Voices

Be - a - ti pa - ci - fi - ci Be - a - ti mun - do cor - de

quo - ni - am i - psi De - um

quo - ni - am i - psi Deum i - psi De - um vi - de - bunt.

Equal Voices

Be - a - ti pa - ci - fi - ci Be - a - ti mun - do cor - de

quo - ni - am i - psi De - um i - psi De - um vi - de - bunt.

6

CRUCEM TUAM

We adore your cross, O Lord, and we praise your resurrection.

Ostinato Chorale

(The upper voice is sung first one or more times in unison, then the second voice is added, and finally, the choir.)

Accompaniment

Keyboard

GLORIA I

Glory to God in the highest.

Ostinato Response

(Equal voices or mixed voices freely distributed over three parts.)

Glo - ri, Glo - ri, Glo - ri - a in ex - cel - sis De - o.

Accompaniment

Keyboard

HOW BLESSED ARE YOU

Ostinato Chorale

Mixed Voices

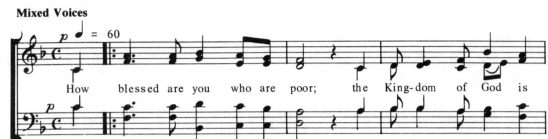

How blessed are you who are poor; the King-dom of God is

yours, how blessed are you who are poor; the King-dom of God is yours.___ How

Equal Voices

How blessed are you who are poor; the King-dom of God is yours, how

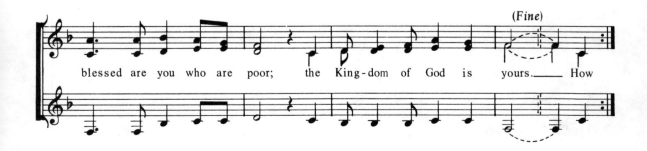

blessed are you who are poor; the King-dom of God is yours.___ How

JESUS, REMEMBER ME

Ostinato Response

Mixed Voices

Je - sus, re - mem-ber me when you come in - to your King - dom.

Je - sus, re - mem-ber me when you come in - to your King - dom.

Equal Voices

Je - sus, re - mem-ber me when you come in - to your King - dom.

Je - sus, re - mem-ber me when you come in - to your King - dom.

Accompaniment

Guitar

Arpeggiated

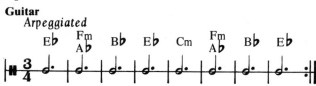

LAUDATE DOMINUM

Praise the Lord, all you peoples.

Ostinato Chorale

Mixed Voices

Lau - da - te Do - mi - num, Lau - da - te Do - mi - num

om - nes gen - tes, Al - le - lu - ia. Al - le - lu - ia.

Equal Voices

Lau - da - te Do - mi - num, Lau - da - te Do - mi - num om - nes

gen - tes, Al - le - lu - ia. Al - le - lu - ia.

Verses   From Psalm 116(117) — with the Chorale

Cantor

Praise the Lord, all you na - tions, praise him all you peo - ples. Al - le - lu - ia. Strong is his love and mer - cy, he is faith - ful for ev - er. Al - le - lu - ia. Al - le - lu - ia, al - le - lu - ia. Let ev - 'ry - thing liv - ing give praise to the Lord. Al - le - praise to the Lord.

LAUDATE OMNES GENTES

All peoples, praise the Lord.

Ostinato Chorale

Mixed Voices

Lau - da - te om - nes gen - tes, lau - da - te Do - mi - num. Lau -

da - te om - nes gen - tes, lau - da - te Do - mi - num! Lau -

Equal Voices

Lau - da - te om - nes gen - tes, lau - da - te Do - mi -

num. Lau - da - te om - nes gen - tes, lau - da - te Do - mi - num! Lau -

MANDATUM NOVUM

I give you a new commandment, says the Lord: Love one another as I have loved you.

Theme

(Ostinato Response or Canon)

Man-da-tum no-vum do— vo-bis, di-cit Do-mi-nus, di-cit Do-mi-nus.—

Accompaniments

Keyboard

Guitar

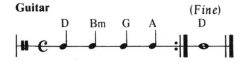

Choir

(hum)

Soprano

1. Verse - Soprano (Solo or Section)

Man-da-tum no-vum do— vo-bis   Man-da-tum no-vum do vo-

bis   ut di-li-ga-tis in-vi-cem   si-cut di-le-xi vos   si-cut di-

le - xi vos, si - cut di - le - xi - vos, di - cit Do - mi - nus,____ di - cit Do - mi -

nus.____

2. Conclusion

A - - - - - - men, A - - - - - - men,____

A - - - - - men, A - - men, A - - - - - - men,

A - - - - - men, A - - - men, A - - - men.

Accompanied Recitative

Keyboard or Instruments

♩ = 69

Cantor

1. Je - sus knew that the hour had come for him to pass from this world to the

2. It was be - fore the feast of the Pass-o - ver, when they were seat-ed at

Fa - ther. He had al-ways loved those in the world who were

sup - per, Je - sus rose from the ta - ble, and poured

his, and would show his love for them right to the end.

wa-ter in-to a ba - sin, and be - gan to wash his dis - ci - ples

feet. Man-da-tum no-vum do___ vo - bis, di - cit Do - mi -

1. Cantor 2. All

nus, di-cit Do-mi-nu(s). 3. Then Je-sus

said: Do you un-der-stand what I have done to you?

What I just did was to give you an ex-am-ple. As I have done, so al-so you must do.

A new com-mand-ment I give to you: Love___ one an-oth-___ er.

Mandatum novum do vobis, dicit Dominus, dicit Dominus.

4. Just as my love has been for you, so must

your love be for each other. This is how all will know that you are my disciples:

by the love that you have for one another.

Repeat the
theme
MANDATUM
NOVUM
above

18

MISERERE MEI

Turn to me, have mercy on me, for I am alone and poor.

Ostinato Response

Mi - se - re - re me - i Do - mi - ne mi - se - re - re.

Canon (ad libitum)

Res - pi - ce in me et mi - se - re - re me - i Quo - ni - am

u - ni - cus et pau - per sum e - go.

Accompaniments

Harp or Guitar

G   D   Em   Bm   C   Am   D   G

Keyboard

Choir

(hum)

Verses From Psalm 24(25)

Cantor

1. Turn to me and have mer - cy for I am lone - ly and poor.

2. See my af - flic - tion see___ my toil and take all my sins a - way.

3. Pre - serve my life and res - cue me for my hope is in you, O Lord.

* Choose either part.

MISERERE NOBIS

Have mercy on us, O Lord.

MISERICORDIAS DOMINI

For ever will I sing the mercy of the Lord.

Ostinato Response

All Two or three Equal Voices

Mi - se - ri - cor - di - as Do - mi - ni in ae - ter - num can - ta - bo.

Accompaniments

Keyboard or Instruments

Guitar

Arpeggiated

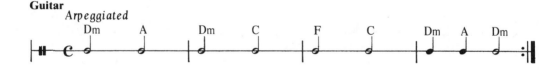

Choir

Verses From Psalm 88(89)

Cantor

1. From age to age through all gen - er - a - tions, my mouth shall pro - claim your

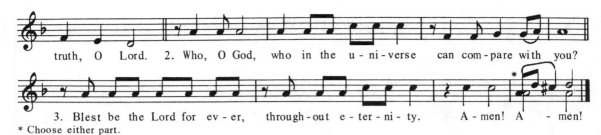

truth, O Lord. 2. Who, O God, who in the u-ni-verse can com-pare with you?

3. Blest be the Lord for ev-er, through-out e-ter-ni-ty. A-men! A-men!

* Choose either part.

Canticle of Simeon
NUNC DIMITTIS

Now, Lord, you can let your servant go in peace according to your promise.

Ostinato Chorale

Mixed Voices

Nunc di-mit-tis ser-vum tu-um Do-mi-ne,_____ se-

Do-mi-ne

(Fine)

Do-mi-ne,

cun-dum ver-bum tu-um in___ pa-ce_____ Nunc di-

Do-mi-ne,

Equal Voices

Nunc di-mit-tis ser-vum tu-um Do-mi-ne,_____ se-

Nunc di-mit tis ser-vum tu-um Do-mi-ne, Do-mi-ne, se-

cun-dum ver-bum tu-um in___ pa-ce._____ (Fine) Nunc di-

cun-dum ver-bum tu-um in pa-ce! Do-mi-ne, Nunc di-

Accompaniment

Guitar (Fine)

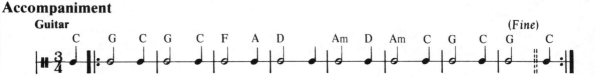

C G C G C F A D Am D Am C G C G C

Lord's Prayer
PATER NOSTER

Our Father In Heaven (I.C.E.T.)

Cantor

Our Fa-ther in heav-en, hal-lowed be your Name, your king-dom come, your will be done, on earth as in heav-en. Give us to-day our dai-ly bread. For-give us our sins as we for-give those who sin a-gainst us. Save us from the time of trial and de-liv-er us from e - vil. For the king-dom, the power, and the glo-ry are yours now and for e - ver. A - - men!

Our Father Who Art In Heaven

Cantor

Our Fa-ther, who art in heav-en, hal-lowed be thy name; thy king-dom come; thy will be done on earth as it is in heav-en. Give us this day___ our dai-ly bread; and for-give us our tres-pass-es as we for-give those who tres-pass a-gainst us; and lead us not in-to temp-ta-tion, but de-liv-er us from e - vil. For the king-dom, the pow'r, and the glo-ry are yours, now and for ev - er. A - - - - men.

Magnificat II
SANCTUM NOMEN DOMINI

My soul magnifies the holy name of the Lord.

Ostinato Chorale
Mixed Voices

San - ctum no - men Do - mi - ni ma - gni - fi - cat a - ni - ma me - a.

San - ctum no - men Do - mi - ni ma - gni - fi - cat a - ni - ma me - a.

Equal Voices

San - ctum no - men Do - mi - ni ma - gni - fi - cat a - ni - ma me - a.

San - ctum no - men Do - mi - ni ma - gni - fi - cat a - ni - ma me - a.

Accompaniment
Keyboard

SURREXIT DOMINUS VERE I

The Lord is truly risen! Christ is risen today!

Easter Chorale

(Can be superimposed on the canon ''Cantate Domino'' with its instrumental parts).

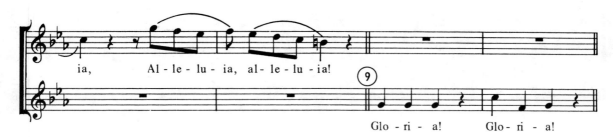

Al-le-lu - ia,   Al-le-lu - ia, al-le-lu-ia, al-le-lu - ia,   Al-le-lu-

re!

ia, al - le - lu - ia!   Sur - re - xit Chris - tus ho - di - e!   Al - le - lu -

ia,   Al - le -lu - ia, al - le - lu - ia, al-le - lu - ia,   Al - le - lu - ia, al - le - lu -ia!

Accompaniments
Keyboard

Guitar I (harmonic pattern)

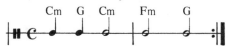

Guitar II

Various instrumental parts for this chorale can be found under the canon "Cantate Domino." (Instrumental edition)

UBI CARITAS

Where charity and love are found, God himself is there.

Ostinato Response

Two or Three Equal Voices

Two Voices / Third Voice ad lib.

U - bi ca - ri - tas___ et a - mor,___ U - bi ca - ri -

tas___ De - us i - bi - est.

Accompaniments

Keyboard or Instruments

Guitar

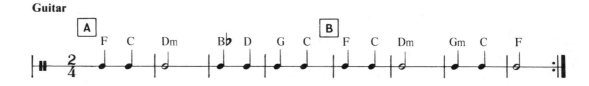

| A | F | C | Dm | Bb | D | G | C | B | F | C | Dm | Gm | C | F |

Bass (Cello, etc.)

Choir

U - bi ca - ri - tas_____ a - mor,_____ U - bi ca - ri -
et a - mor,_____

tas,_____ De - us i - bi est.

Verses B

Cantor B

1. Your love, O Je - sus Christ, has gath - ered us to - geth - er.

2. May your love, O Je - sus Christ, be fore - most in our lives.

3. Let us love one an - oth - er as God has loved_____ us.

4. Let us be one in love to - geth - er in the one bread of Christ.

5. The love of God in Je - sus Christ bears e - ter - nal joy.

6. The love of God in Je - sus Christ will nev - er have an end.

* Choose either part.

Verses [C] 1 and [C] 2 **Cantor** and Accompaniment

All

(Conclusion of [B])　　　　　[C] 1　　　　　　　begin [A]

TACET　　etc.

(. . De-us i - bi -est)

Cantor

[C] 1

1. It is your love, O Je-sus Christ, which gath-ers us to - geth-er.

Cantor

3. The love of God in Je-sus Christ sur-pass - es ev-'ry- thing.

Cantor

5. It is your love, O Je-sus Christ, that brings us to joy e - ter-nal.

Cantor

7. O Lord, keep us as one, sus - tain us in your love.

Guitar

Gm　C　F　Am　E　Am　F　Bb　C　F

Keyboard or Instruments

(Conclusion of [B])　　[C] 1　　　　begin [A]　etc.

* Choose either part.

Accompaniments - for the Refrain [A] [B]

Guitar

[A] F C Dm Bb D G C [B] F C Dm Gm C F

Keyboard or Instruments

[A]　　　　　　　　[B]　　　　　[C] 1 or [C] 2

p　　　p

(Conclusion of **B**) **C** 2   begin **A**

All

(. . De-us i - bi - est)

Cantor

2. O Lord,___ in your great love   re - move   all our sins.

Cantor

4. God's love re-vealed in Je - sus Christ   will nev-er come to end.

Cantor

6. Let us be   one   in love to - geth -er   in the   one   bread of Christ.

Cantor

8. Lord, in the eve-ning of our lives   we shall find   you a - gain.

Guitar

Gm   C   F   D   Gm   D   Gm   F   etc.

Keyboard or Instruments

Accompanied Recitative

Guitar *Freely arpeggiated*
F

Cantor *Calmly*

1. If I have the gift   of prophesy, understanding all the mysteries there are, know-ing

Keyboard or Instruments or Choir (hum)

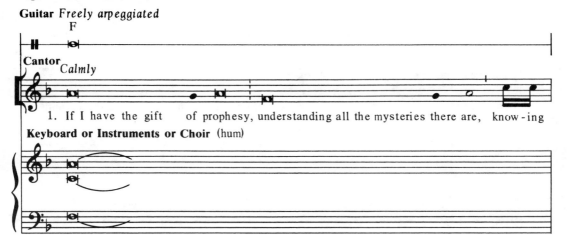

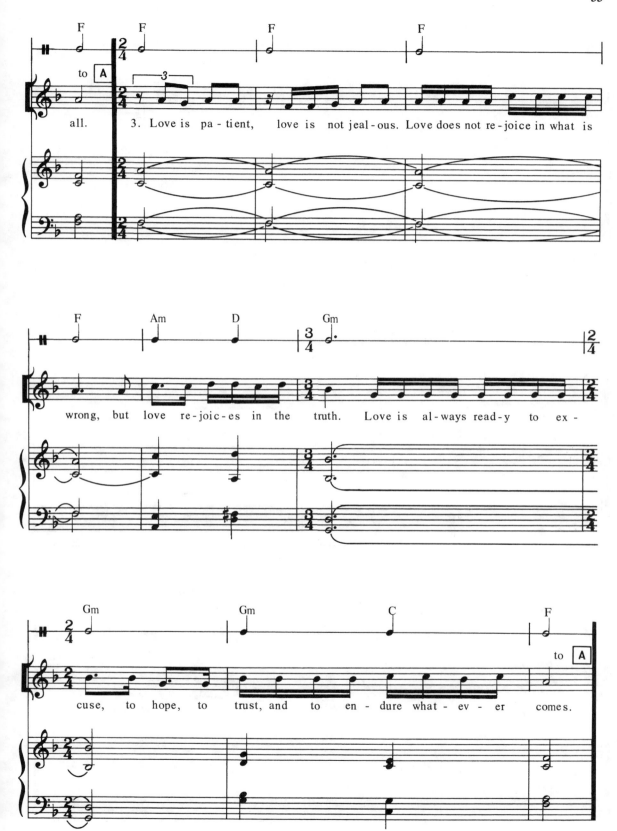

all. 3. Love is pa - tient, love is not jeal - ous. Love does not re - joice in what is

wrong, but love re - joic - es in the truth. Love is al - ways read - y to ex -

cuse, to hope, to trust, and to en - dure what - ev - er comes.

4. Love nev-er fails. Prophesies will cease, and tongues will be si - lent,

know-ledge will pass a - way; but there are on - ly three things in the

end that last: faith, hope and love, and the great-est of these is love.

Verses A B For small mixed choir or 4 cantors.

The love of Christ has gathered us into one.
 Where charity and love are found, God is there.
Let us exult in him and be glad.
 Where...

Let us love one another with sincere hearts.
 Where...
And may Christ, our God, dwell in our midst.
 Where...

Mixed Voices

1. Con - gre - ga - vit nos in u - num Chri - sti a - mor.__ U - bi ca - ri - tas et a - mor,
2. ℣ Ex cor - de di - li - ga - mus nos sin - ce - ro.__ U - bi ca - ri - tas et a - mor,

De - us i - bi est. Ex - ul - te - mus et in ip - so iu - cun - de - mur.__
De - us i - bi est. Et in me - di - o nos - tri sit Chri - stus De - us.__

U - bi ca - ri - tas et a - mor, De - us i - bi est.
U - bi ca - ri - tas et a - mor, De - us i - bi est.

36

VENI SANCTE SPIRITUS
Come, Holy Spirit

Ostinato Response

All

Ve - ni Sanc - te Spi - ri - tus.___

Women's Voices

Ve - ni Sanc - te Spi - ri - tus.___

Mixed Voices and Accompaniment

Ve - ni Sanc - te Spi - ri - tus.___

Men's Voices

Ve - ni Sanc - te Spi - ri - tus.___

To begin this ostinato, the four mixed voices should make their entrances in the following order:

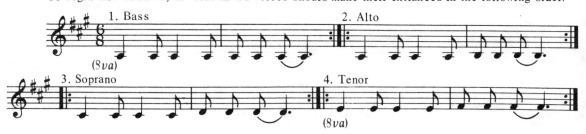

Accompaniment

Guitar

Verses

As the ostinato continues, vocal and instrumental verses are sung or played as desired with some space always left between the verses (after the cantor's "Veni Sancte Spiritus").

Cantor

1. Come, Ho-ly Spir-it,__ from heav-en shine__ forth with your glo-rious light.

Ve-ni San-cte Spi-ri-tus.__ 2. Come, Fa-ther__ of the poor, come, gen-er-ous

Spir-it,__ come, light of our hearts.____ Ve-ni San-cte Spi-ri-tus.__

1. Come from the four winds, O Spir-it, come breath of God;__ dis-

perse the shad-ows ov-er us, re-new and strength-en your peo-ple.__

Ve-ni San-cte Spi-ri-tus.__ 2. Fa-ther__ of the poor come__ to our pov-er-ty.__

Show-er up-on us the sev-en gifts of your grace. Be the light of our lives__ oh

come. Ve-ni San-cte Spi-ri-tus.__ 3. You are our on-ly com-fort-er,__

Peace__ of the soul. In the heat you shade us; in our la-bor__ you re-

fresh us,__ and in trou-ble you are our strength. Ve-ni San-cte

Spi - ri - tus.___ 4. Kin - dle in our hearts the flame of your love that in the dark - ness___

___ of the world it may glow and reach to all___ for ev - er.___ Ve - ni..

* Choose either part.

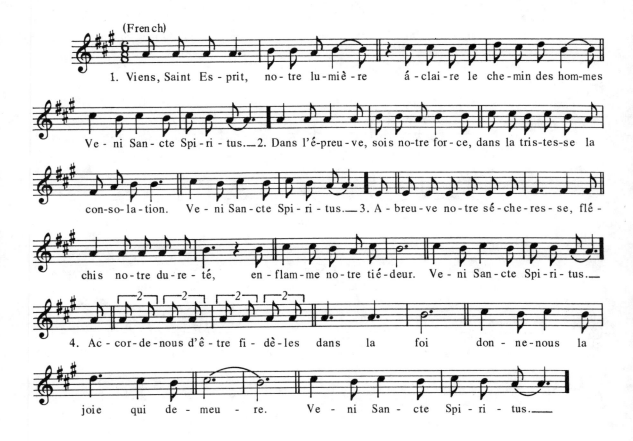

(French)

1. Viens, Saint Es - prit, no - tre lu - miè - re á - clai - re le che - min des hom - mes

Ve - ni San - cte Spi - ri - tus.___2. Dans l'é - preu - ve, sois no - tre for - ce, dans la tris - tes - se la

con - so - la - tion. Ve - ni San - cte Spi - ri - tus.___3. A - breu - ve no - tre sé - che - res - se, flé -

chis no - tre du - re - té, en - flam - me no - tre tié - deur. Ve - ni San - cte Spi - ri - tus.___

4. Ac - cor - de - nous d'ê - tre fi - dè - les dans la foi don - ne - nous la

joie qui de - meu - re. Ve - ni San - cte Spi - ri - tus.___

(German)

1. Komm, Hei - li - ger Geist, lass den Glanz dei - ner Herr - lich - keit vom

Him-mel er-strah - - len. Ve - ni San - cte Spi - ri - tus.— 2. Komm, Va-ter der

Ar - men, Komm, Ur-sprung al - ler Ga-ben, Komm, Licht der Her - zen. Ve - ni..

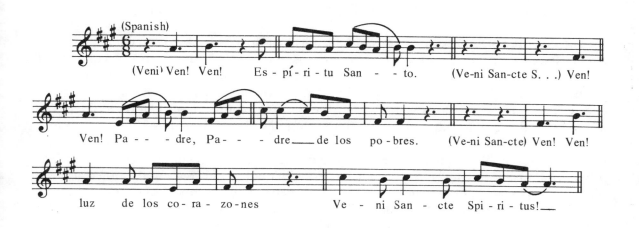

(Spanish)

(Veni) Ven! Ven! Es - pí - ri - tu San - - to. (Ve-ni San-cte S. . .) Ven!

Ven! Pa - - dre, Pa - - dre — de los po - bres. (Ve-ni San-cte) Ven! Ven!

luz de los co - ra - zo - nes Ve - ni San - cte Spi - ri - tus!—

(Italian)

1. Vie - ni San - to Spi - ri - to — riem-pi i cuo-ri dei tuoi fe-de-li

e ac-cen-di in es-si il fuo-co del tu - o — a - mo - re. Ve - ni San - cte

Spi - ri - tus.— 2. Con-so - la - to - re per-fet - - to; os-pi-te mi - te dell'

a - ni - ma; dol-cis - si - mo sol-lie - vo. Ve - ni San - cte Spi - ri - tus.—

II

LITANIES AND OTHER TEXTS WITH REFRAINS

In the preceding pieces, the English text of the verses (of the psalms, the Beatitudes, the Lord's Prayer, etc.) were superimposed upon the continuous repetition of a response. In this group, however, the verses $\boxed{A}$ are sung *between* very short phrases $\boxed{B}$ which act as refrains. These verses are sustained by harmonies composed of only a few chords that are either hummed or vocalized by the choir, and, if possible, by the assembly.

In some of the pieces, both the text and the music of the verses have been completely written out (e.g., *Adoramus te, Libera nos Domine, Maranatha! Alleluia! I* etc.). In contrast, all the settings of the *Kyrie eleison* and similar refrains *(Domine miserere, Exaudi nos, O Christe audi nos, Veni lumen cordium)* allow the use of verses taken from various liturgical and scriptural texts, or verses which arise from the free expression of petition in the prayer of the faithful. The final chord of the refrain is hummed by choir and assembly, for as long as is necessary. Each singer breathes in a random fashion, ensuring that the sound of the chord remains stable. Over this layer of sound, the cantors proclaim the texts in free improvisation, using the notes of the chord as principal notes and treating the other notes of the scale as passing tones. In most instances, the verses will finish with a change of chord. This should be announced and prepared by a small melodic formula in the final words of the cantor's part (for example, *Lord, have mercy* or *Hear us, we pray,* etc.) leading to that final chord, after which the refrain is repeated, and so on to the end of the piece. It is clear that both close attention to the accentuation of the text and a musical sensitivity are demanded to evoke the spiritual value of this type of litany.

SPECIAL CASES

Adoramus te Domine I
An accompaniment in parallel octaves and fifths underlines the ancient style of this piece. A low-pitched percussion instrument (timpani tuned to A or a gong) should maintain a regular pulse.

Adoramus te Domine II
If the refrain *Gloria* is used instead of the *Adoramus* or *Lord we worship you,* the style of the piece changes completely. The three *Glorias* should ring out like a carillon, lightly and in a somewhat quicker tempo.

Credo I
The first version is a setting of the Apostles' Creed in which all the words of the text are notated for a two-part ensemble (choir or a small group of soloists). A second version allows a cantor to sing in free psalmody another text (e.g., the Nicene Creed), over the harmonic support of the final chord of the refrain.

Maranatha! Alleluia! I
The refrains are designed for two voices (men and women mixed). They finish on an open chord of octaves and fifths which should be held by humming softly. The soloists sing their verses freely over this foundation; but their final notes should be well marked rhythmically in the tempo of the following refrain which should break out strong.

Memento nostri Domine

Unlike other pieces in this collection, this setting includes a series of flute obbligati which are an integral part of the composition. Each of its eight sections has the following pattern: *flute, solo voice, response* (given first by the soloist and then repeated by all and followed by a brief silence). The use of this very simple form gives an intense expression to the believer's meditation. The quality of interpretation is all the more important since the musical means are quite basic.

Veni Creator Spiritus

The English verses provided form a collection of texts and melodic patterns. Other texts may be adapted from this model, particularly by using other languages to evoke more clearly the event of Pentecost.

English recitatives

Refer to the preceding section for the two pieces *Mandatum novum* and *Ubi caritas*. The themes of these ostinato *responses* may also be used as *refrains* to conclude a cantor's solo (recitative or verse).

ADORAMUS TE DOMINE I

We adore you, O Lord.

1. O crucified Jesus, conceived by the Holy Spirit,

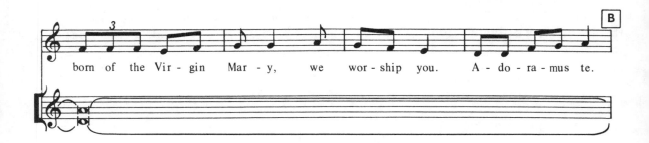

born of the Virgin Mary, we worship you. A-do-ra-mus te.

Guitar or Low Percussion   Gong, Timpani, etc.

   etc.   (Regular pulse on a low A without chord)

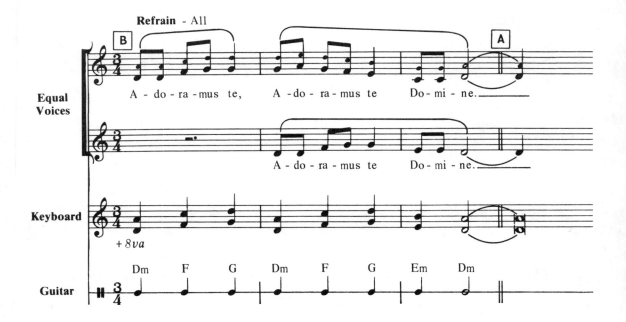

43

Mixed Voices

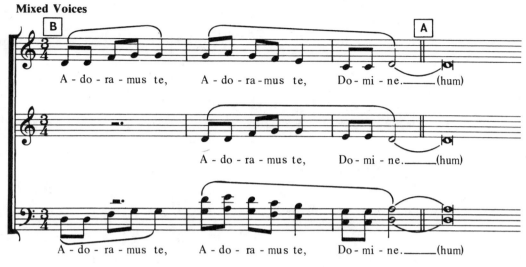

Verses

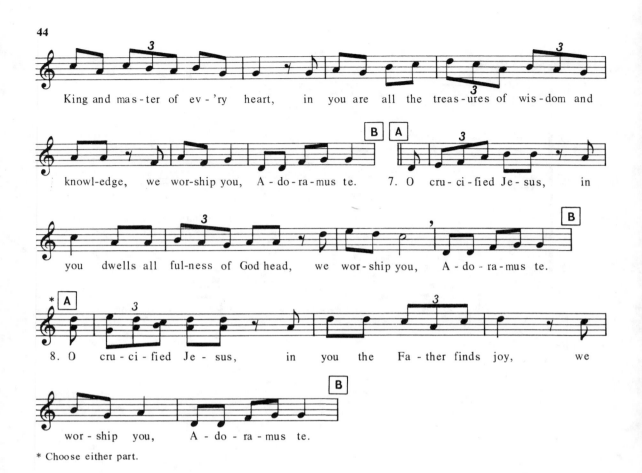

King and mas-ter of ev-'ry heart, in you are all the treas-ures of wis-dom and

knowl-edge, we wor-ship you, A - do - ra - mus te. 7. O cru - ci - fied Je - sus, in

you dwells all ful-ness of God head, we wor-ship you, A - do - ra - mus te.

8. O cru - ci - fied Je - sus, in you the Fa - ther finds joy, we

wor - ship you, A - do - ra - mus te.

* Choose either part.

ADORAMUS TE DOMINE II — GLORIA

We adore you, O Lord. — Glory to God in the highest.

Equal Voices

(hum) A - do - ra - mus te Do - mi - ne.

Mixed Voices

(hum) A - do - ra - mus te Do - mi - ne.

Alternate Refrains

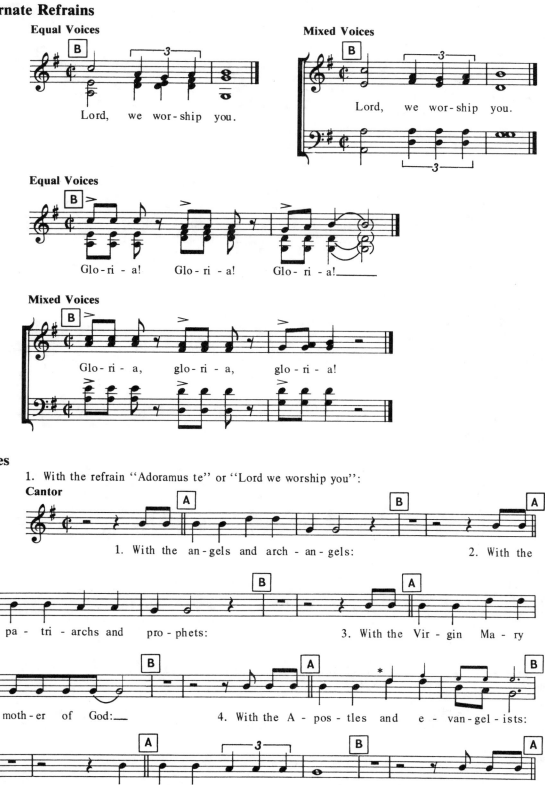

Verses

1. With the refrain "Adoramus te" or "Lord we worship you":

* Choose either part.

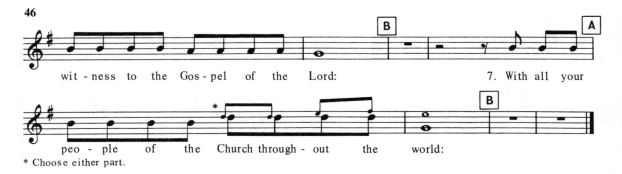

wit - ness to the Gos - pel of the Lord: 7. With all your

peo - ple of the Church through - out the world:

* Choose either part.

2. With the refrain "Gloria Gloria" and trumpet (see instrumental volume).

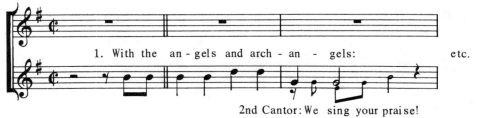

1. With the an - gels and arch - an - gels: etc.

2nd Cantor: We sing your praise!

Choral Variation (hummed or with text)

Glo - ri - a, Glo - ri - a in ex - cel - sis Deo,

Glo - ri - a, Glo - ri - a, Al - le - lu -

Glo - ri - a in ex - cel - sis De - o,

Glo - ri - a, Glo - ri - a,

Glo - ri - a, Glo - ri - a, Al - le - lu - ia, Glo - ri,

ia, Glo - ri - a, Al - le - lu - ia,

Glo - ri - a, Al - le - lu - ia, Glo - ri,

Glo - ri - a, Glo - ri - a,

CREDO I

We believe in one God, in one Lord, in one Spirit.

Refrain

* 1st time: Dominum; 2nd time: Spiritum.

The Apostle's Creed

Cantors or Choir (a cappella)
Freely and animated

1. I be-lieve in God, the Fa-ther al-might-y, cre-a-tor of heav-en and earth.

2. I be-lieve in Je-sus Christ, his on-ly Son, our Lord. He was con-ceived by the pow'r of the Ho-ly Spir-it and born of the Vir-gin Ma-ry. *Refrain*

3. He suf-fered un-der Pon-tius Pi-late, was cru-ci-fied, died and was bur-ied. He de-scend-ed to the dead. *Refrain*

4. On the third day he rose a-gain. He as-cend-ed in-to heav-en, and is seat-ed at the right hand of the Fa-ther. He will come a-gain to judge the liv-ing and the dead. *Refrain*

5. I be-lieve in the Ho-ly Spir-it, the ho-ly cath-'lic Church, the com-mun-ion of saints, the for-give-ness of sins, the res-ur-rec-tion of the bod-y, and the life ev-er-last-ing. *Refrain*

Alternate Formula for Verses

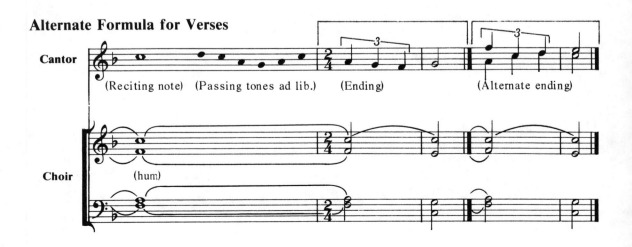

Cantor
(Reciting note) (Passing tones ad lib.) (Ending) (Alternate ending)

Choir
(hum)

DOMINE MISERERE I-II

Lord, have mercy on us.

Domine Miserere 1

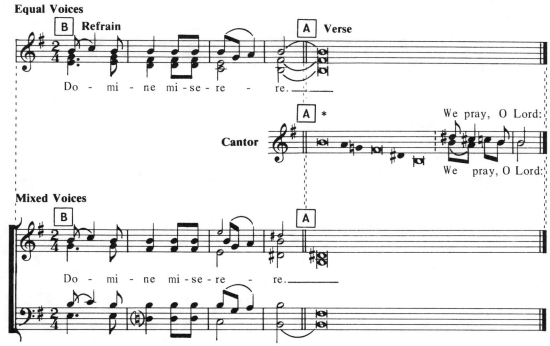

Domine Miserere 2

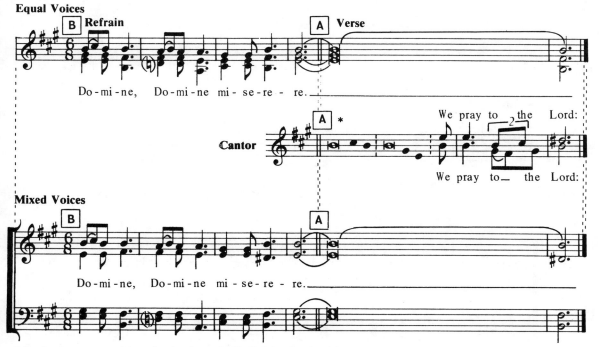

* Psalm verses or petitions freely chanted. To finish, choose either part.

EXAUDI NOS

Hear us

Accompaniments

GLORIA TIBI DOMINE

Glory to you, O Lord.

Refrain - All

Equal Voices

Glo - ri - a ti - bi Do - mi - ne, Glo - ri - a ti - bi Do - mi - ne,

Glo - ri - a ti - bi Do - mi - ne.

Mixed Voices

Glo - ri - a ti - bi Do - mi - ne,

Accompaniments

Keyboard

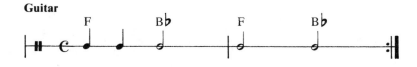

Guitar

F   Bb   F   Bb

Choir

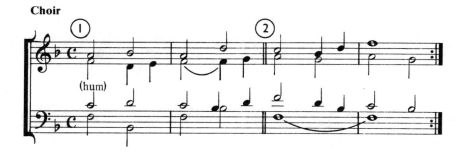

(hum)

52

Choir in Canon

Glo - ri - a ti - bi Do -mi -ne, Do - mi - ne, Glo - ri - a ti -

bi Do -mi - ne, Do - mi - ne.

Verses - with B

Cantor

O Je - sus, Son of God: O Je - sus splen -dor of the

Fa - ther: O Je - sus, light e - ter - nal: King of glo - ry and Son of

jus - tice: Born of the Vir - gin Mar - y: O Je - sus, Won -der -ful

coun - sel - lor: Strong Lord, e - ter - nal God: O Je - sus, Prince of peace: O

gen -tle and hum -ble of heart: Lov -ing all the pure in heart: O Je - sus, God of

peace: O Je - sus, friend of all: O Je - sus, source of life: O

Je - sus mod - el of ho - li - ness: O Je - sus, broth - er of the poor, O

Je - sus, Good Shep -herd, true light, our Way and our Life: O

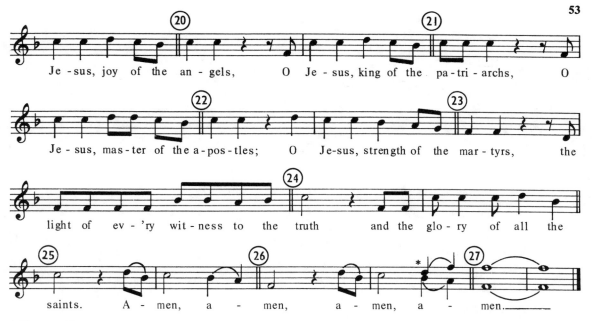

Je -sus, joy of the an -gels, O Je -sus, king of the pa -tri -archs, O Je -sus, mas -ter of the a -pos -tles; O Je -sus, strength of the mar -tyrs, the light of ev -'ry wit -ness to the truth and the glo -ry of all the saints. A -men, a - men, a - men, a - men.

* Choose either part.

JESU CHRISTE MISERERE

Jesus Christ have mercy on us.

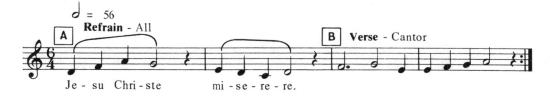

Je - su Chri - ste mi - se - re - re.

Accompaniments

Keyboard or Instruments

Guitar

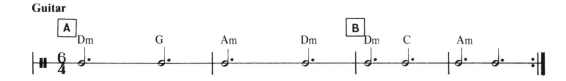

Treble Voices

Je - su Chri - ste   mi - se - re - re   (hum)

Mixed Voices

Je - su Chri - ste   mi - se - re - re   (hum)

Verses - with [B]

Cantor Penitential Rite

1. You raise the dead to life in the Spir - it:

2. You___ bring par - don and peace to the sin - ner: 3. You bring light to

those___ in dark - ness:

Cantor Psalm 24

1. To you, O Lord, I lift up my soul.   2. In you I trust,

keep me from shame.   3. Your ways, O Lord, make known to me.   4. Guide me in your

truth___ and teach me.   5. In your kind - ness re - mem - ber me.

* Choose either part.

KYRIE ELEISON I-X

Lord, have mercy.

Kyrie 1

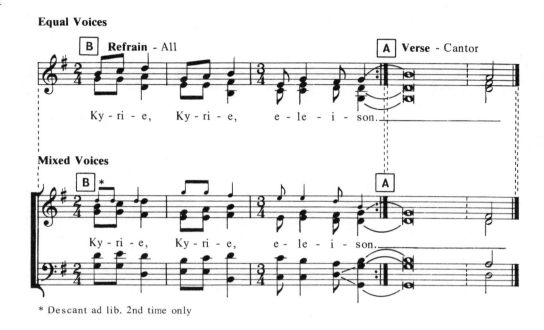

* Descant ad lib. 2nd time only

Kyrie 2

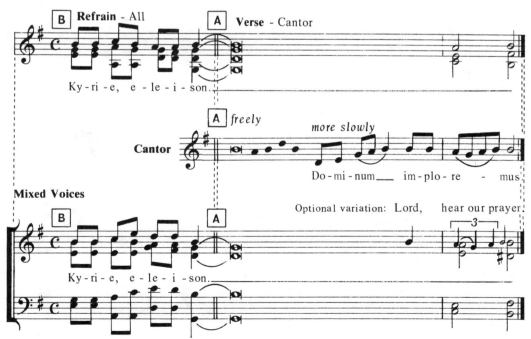

Kyrie 3

Equal Voices

Ky - ri - e e - le - i - son, E - le - i - son.

Mixed Voices

Ky - ri - e e - le - i - son, E - le - i - son.

Kyrie 4

Equal Voices (or Mixed Voices with Tenors and Basses singing lower line.)

Ky - ri - e e - le - i - son, e - le - i - son.

Mixed Voices

Ky - ri - e e - le - i - son, e - le - i - son.

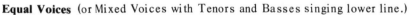

Kyrie 5

Kyrie 6

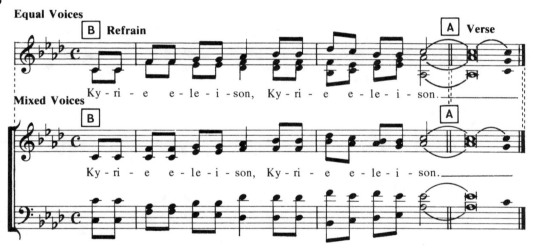

Kyrie 7

58

Kyrie 8

Kyrie 9

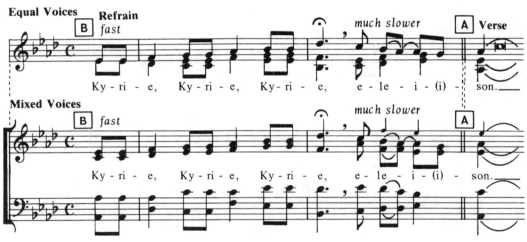

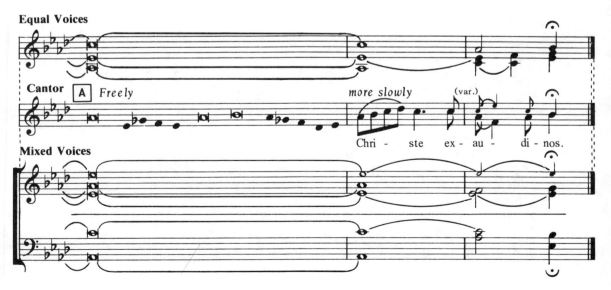

Kyrie 10

Equal Voices

Mixed Voices

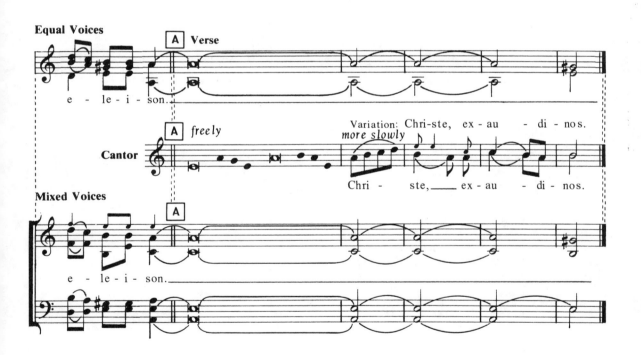

LIBERA NOS DOMINE

Deliver us, O Lord.

Li - be - ra nos Do - mi - ne.   Li - be - ra nos Do - mi - ne.

Accompaniments

Keyboard

Guitar

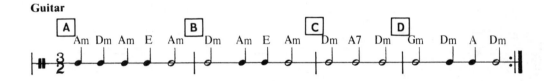

Equal Voices

(hum)   Li - be - ra nos Do - mi - ne.   (hum)

Li - be - ra nos Do - mi - ne.

Mixed Voices

(hum)   Li - be - ra nos Do - mi - ne,   (hum)

Li – be – ra nos Do – mi – ne,

Verses

Cantor

1. Li – be – ra nos Do – mi – ne: Let us im – plore the mer – cy of the Lord:

2. God of kind – ness and com – pas – sion: From in – jus – tice and ha – tred:

3. From war and fam – ine: From dis – ease and dis – as – ter:

4. By the mys – t'ry of your in – car – na – tion: By your com – ing in – to the world:

5. By your birth in pov – er – ty: By your fast – ing in the des – ert:

6. By your cross and pas – sion: By your res – ur – rec – tion from the dead:

7. By your Ho – ly Spir – it the com – fort – er: and on the Day of Judge – ment:

8. We are sin – ners give us par – don: Give us true re – pent – ance of heart:

MARANATHA! ALLELUIA! I

Come soon! Alleluia!

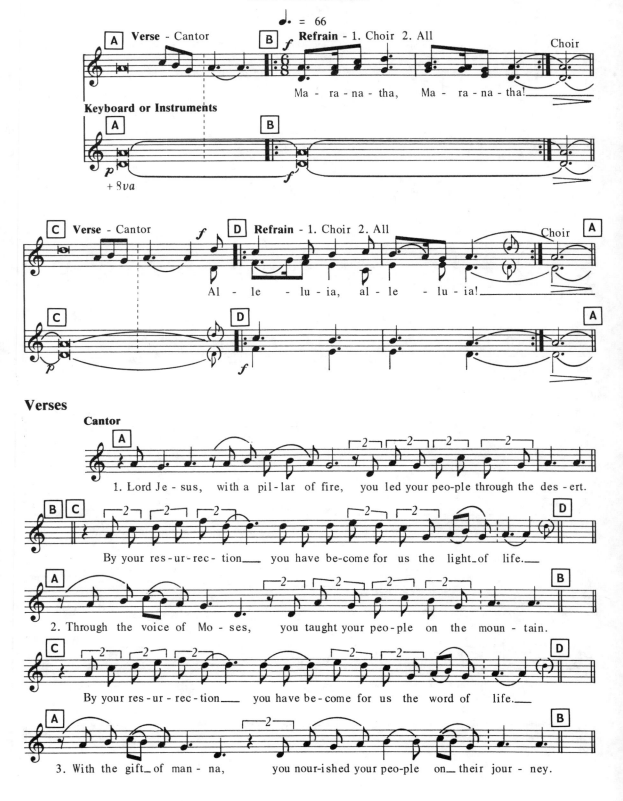

By your res-ur-rec-tion___ you have be-come for us the bread__ of life.___

4. With wa-ter from__ the rock, you gave your peo-ple drink.___

By your res-ur-rec-tion___ you have giv-en us the Spir-it of life.___

MEMENTO NOSTRI DOMINE

Remember us, O Lord.

Flute Solo
Calmly ♩ = 72

1. Let us think on Je-sus the Lord: in-stead of the joy meant for him

he en-dured the cross, ig-nor-ing its dis-grace. Me-men-to no-stri Do-mi-ne.

A Verse - Cantor

B Refrain - 1. Cantor, 2. All

Flute Solo
A little faster

rall.

A Verse

2. O Jesus Christ, the King of glo-ry, you were born in humility to confound the proud

B Refrain

and to raise the hum-ble. Me-men-to no-stri Do-mi-ne.

64

Flute Solo

Calmly

3

A Verse

3. You lived among us, healing the sick, proclaiming the good news to the poor,

B Refrain

and free-dom to pris-on-ers. Me-men-to no-stri Do-mi-ne.

Flute Solo

Faster   *rall.*

4

(echo)

A Verse

4. You came to loose the chains of ev-'ry kind of slav-er-y,

B Refrain

friend of the lowly, bread of hungry souls. Me-men-to no-stri Do-mi-ne.

Flute Solo

Calmly

5

very slow   **A** Verse

5. Je-sus, master of patience and good-ness,

B Refrain

for-giv-ing all who seek your mer-cy. Me-men-to no-stri Do-mi-ne.

Flute Solo

A little faster

6

A Verse

6. Je - sus, gentle and hum - ble of heart, call - ing the wea - ry and the bur - dened.

B Refrain

Me - men - to no - stri Do - mi - ne.

Flute Solo

Calmly

7

p

A Verse

7. Jesus, you came into the world to serve and to lay down your life

you had no - where to lay your head, you were be - trayed for mon - ey,

B Refrain

dragged before Pi - late and nailed to the cross. Me - men - to no - stri Do - mi - ne.

Flute Solo

A little more movement

8

f

p (echo)

ff

A Verse

8. Je - sus, by your resurrection

from the dead, you are Lord of all the worlds a - live for ever to

B Refrain

intercede with your Fa - ther and ours. Me - men - to no - stri Do - mi - ne.

Me - men - to no - stri Do - mi - ne. Me - men - to no - stri Do - mi - ne.

O CHRISTE AUDI NOS

O Christ, hear us.

Equal Voices

[B] **Refrain - All**   [A] **Verse**

O Chri - ste au - di - nos.
Hear us, O Christ, Our Lord.

[A] *freely*

Cantor

Mixed Voices

[B]   [A]

O Chri - ste au - di - nos.
Hear us, O Christ, Our Lord.

TE ROGAMUS AUDI NOS

We ask you to hear us.

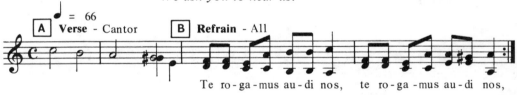

♩ = 66

[A] **Verse - Cantor**   [B] **Refrain - All**

Te ro - ga - mus au - di nos, te ro - ga - mus au - di nos,

Accompaniments

Keyboard

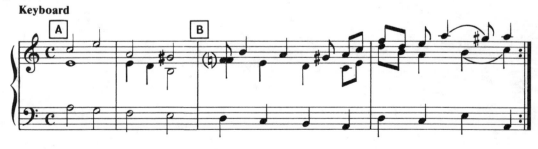

[A]   [B]

Guitar

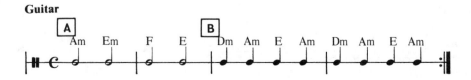

[A]   Am   Em   F   E   [B]   Dm   Am   E   Am   Dm   Am   E   Am

VENI CREATOR SPIRITUS

Come, Creator Spirit

Verse

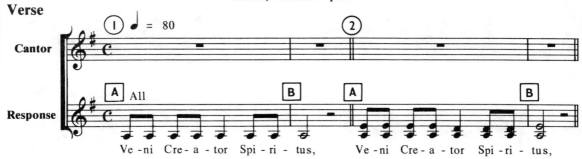

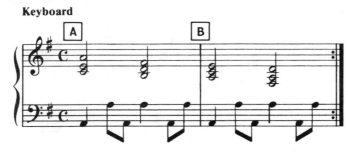

Accompaniments

Keyboard

Guitar

Am Bm7 Am D

Choir

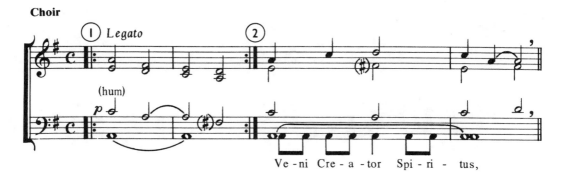

Ve - ni Cre - a - tor Spi - ri - tus, sim.

Verses - with [B]
Cantor

1. Come, Spir - it cre - a - tor. 2. Come, Fa - ther of the poor.

3. Come, gen - er - ous Spir - it. 4. Come, light of our hearts. 5. Come source of

* Choose either part.

life. 6. Come, with your sev-en-fold gifts. 7. O Spir-it of wis-dom.

8. O Spir-it of in-tel-li-gence. 9. O Spir-it of coun-cil.

10. O Spir-it of pow'r. 11. O Spir-it of knowl-edge. 12. O Spir-it of

pi-e-ty. 13. O Spir-it of o-be-di-ence. 14. En-light-en us with your

light. 15. Fill us with your love. 16. Strength-en us with your pow'r.

17. A - - men. 18. A - men. 19. A - men.

VENI LUMEN CORDIUM I-II

Come, light of our hearts. Come, Holy Spirit.

Veni Lumen Cordium 1

Equal Voices

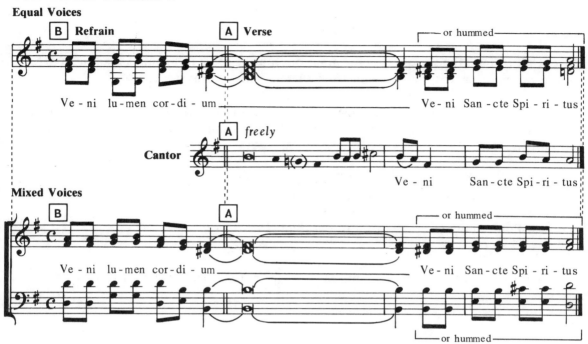

Veni Lumen Cordium 2

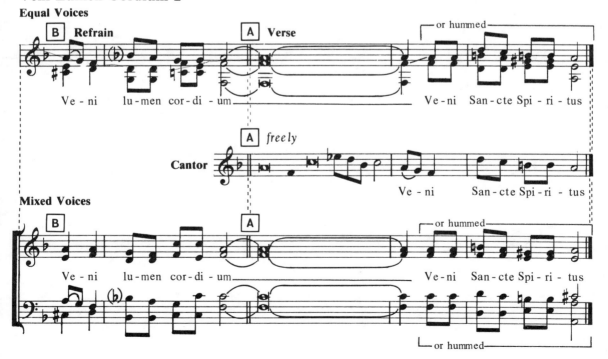

III

ACCLAMATIONS

Depending upon their text, these acclamations may be used following a reading, a passage from a psalm, a prayer, or a section from the eucharistic prayer, etc.

They may also be treated as *refrains*: the final chord is held by humming as in the case of the *Kyrie eleison* and the other short litany refrains, while a cantor improvises upon the chosen text:

- verses from a psalm of praise, with an *Alleluia,*
- petitions in the Lord's Prayer, with an *Amen,*
- an Advent text, with a *Maranatha,*
- a Palm Sunday text, with *Hosanna Filio David,*
- and so on.

In each of the Alleluias, the intonation for the cantor is sung the first time only.

ALLELUIAS I-VI

Alleluia 1

Equal Voices

Al - le - lu - ia,   Al - le - lu - ia,   Al - le - lu - ia!

Al - le - lu - ia,   Al - le - lu - ia!

Mixed Voices

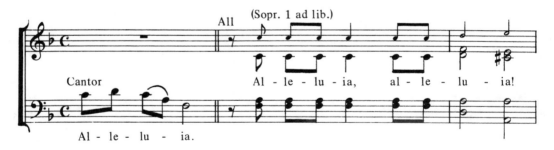

(Sopr. 1 ad lib.)

Al - le - lu - ia,   al - le - lu - ia!

Al - le - lu - ia.

Al - le - lu - ia,   al - le - lu - ia!

Alleluia 2

Equal Voices

Alleluia 3

Equal Voices

Alleluia 4

Equal Voices

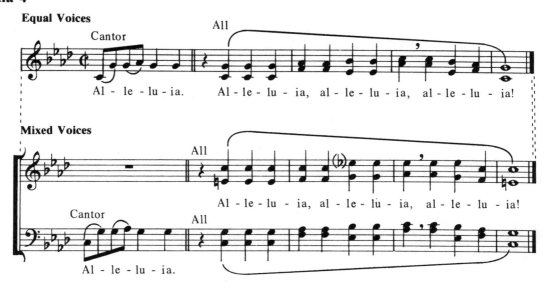

Formulas for chanting verses over sustained final chord of Alleluia.

Alto or Baritone

Soprano or Tenor

* Choose either part.

Alleluia 5

Alleluia 6

AMENS I-III

Amen 1

Amen 2

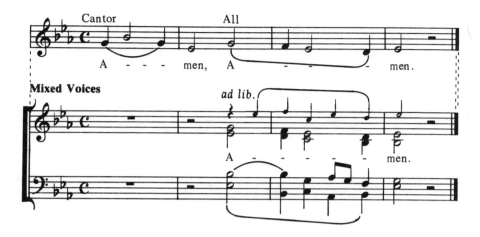

Amen 3

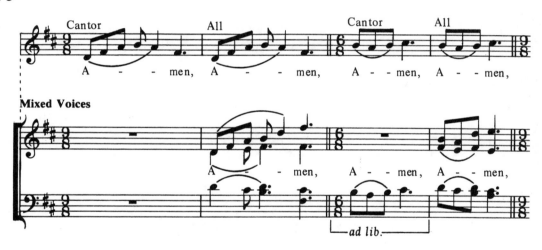

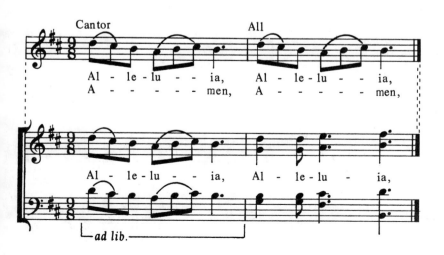

HOSANNA FILIO DAVID

Hosanna to the Son of David.

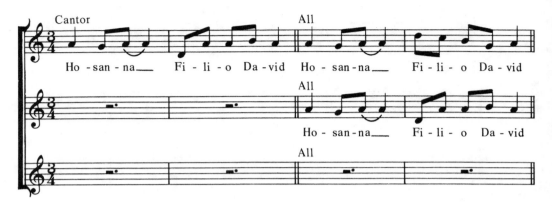

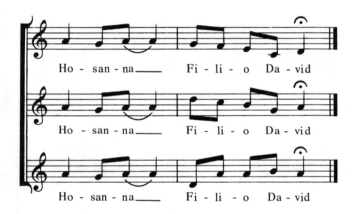

MARANATHA — ALLELUIA II

Come soon! Alleluia!

MARANATHA — VENI DOMINE

Come soon. Come, Lord, and do not delay.

Ma-ra-na-tha, ma-ra-na-tha, Ve-ni Do-mi-ne, No-li tar-da-re.

Mixed Voices

Ve-ni Do-mi-ne, No-li tar-da-re.

MYSTERIUM FIDEI

The mystery of faith. Savior of the world, save us. By your cross and your resurrection you have delivered us.

1. Mys-te-ri-um fi-de-i, mys-te-ri-um fi-de-i.

Choir: S+T
A+B

2. Sal-va-tor mun-di sal-va-nos Mys-te-ri-um fi-de-i.

3. Per cru-cem tu-am li-be-ra-sti nos Mys-te-ri-um fi-de-i.

4. Per re-sur-rec-ti-o-nem tu-am li-be-ra-sti nos Mys-te-ri-um...

SANCTUS DOMINUS
Holy Lord

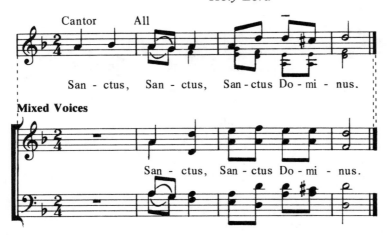

TU SOLUS SANCTUS I-II
You alone are Holy, you alone are Lord, you alone, O Jesus Christ, are Most High.

Tu Solus Sanctus 1

Tu Solus Sanctus 2

tis - si - mus   Je - su   Chri - ste.

Je - su   Chri - ste.

UNUM CORPUS
One Body and one Spirit.

U - num   Cor - pus   et   u - nus   Spi - ri - tus.

Mixed Voices

et   u - nus   Spi - ri - tus.

IV

CANONS

The melodic theme of each canon is based on a simple harmonic pattern (see the Instrumental Edition), and can be used in a variety of ways, from the simplest to the more complex.

1 Theme repeated by all in unison

The principles outlined for the performance of responses and chorales in *ostinato* form also apply here. Varied musical colorings can be given to the repetition of the theme either by adding accompaniments (choir humming, instruments) or by employing simpler means: different vocal timbres in succession (male voices, then female voices), or varying the dynamics level (piano, forte, etc.)

2 Two-part canon

The most usual form of this type of canon is found in *Jubilate, servite* where the second voice follows the first at a measure's distance, like a 'hunt' or 'chase'. This hunting image is traditional: such terms as *caccia* (Italian) or *caza* (Spanish) were used in the past to designate canons. If, for example, the men's voices begin the first part and the women sing the second (or vice versa) the canon will sound clearer because of the differences in pitch and tone-color in the two types of voices.

All of the canons can be sung in this way, even if they are intended for three or four voices (the majority) or even for six (*Per crucem*). A choice will have to be made in these cases as to the point at which the second voice should enter. The structure of the melody will dictate which of the possibilities is best.

In most cases, the second part will enter when the first part has reached letter (B). For example in the *Magnificat:*

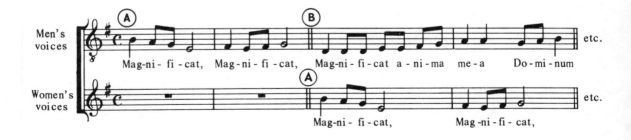

In other cases, a different choice will be made. In the *Veni Creator Spiritus*, for example, the two halves of the melody complement each other in direction — the first half (A)(B) in a descending motion, and the second (C)(D), ascending. In this case the second voice will enter when the first has reached letter (C).

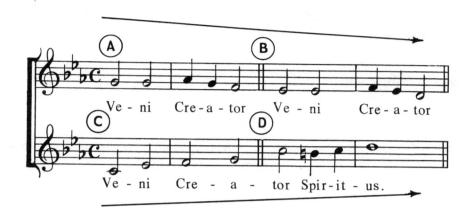

This option makes the conclusion of the canon a simple matter since the two parts can be stopped when they reach the octave D. Other choices are possible, provided that the entries and the progress of the piece are well in control.

3   Canon for three parts and more

In practice, these more complex versions should be kept for a choral group under a conductor who can give clear entries, maintain a steady tempo that avoids speeding-up or slowing-down by the assembly, and is able to bring the canon to a close when desired, with a *fermata* (pause) on the final chord.

But in liturgical usage, the chief role always falls to the assembly. The choir supports the people by singing the first voice with them, and if necessary the second. When the two-part canon is satisfactorily managed, the choir can add the third and fourth parts.

The harmony may also be enriched and a *crescendo* effect may be produced by adding, at the desired moment, an extra accompaniment from a small four-part choral group (singing the choral sequence that is provided for each canon). This could also be the signal for the conclusion.

Guidelines for preparing a scheme that gives the progressive structure of a fuller canon will be found in the special introduction in the Instrumental Edition.

SPECIAL CASES

Agnus Dei

For a simple liturgical version: the theme is sung three times in unison with *miserere nobis* twice, and *dona nobis pacem* the third time.

As a canon, it is preferable to have the assembly sing the last part (D) of the theme in *ostinato*, and the complete melody in canon by the choir.

Benedicite Domino

The canon should finish on the D major chord in the first measure with, for example, an *Amen* (which may conclude a solo sporano verse).

Cantate Domino (and other canons in this series)

Since all these canons are based on the same harmonic pattern, any or all of them may be combined, e.g., the canon in English, *Glory to the Father,* with the Christmas melody, *Gloria 2.* One can be sung by unison men's voices, and the other by unison women's voices; or, each of these groups can sing in two-part canon; etc.

Christus vincit (or **Jubilate coeli**)

The two themes can each be sung in unison, by two different groups of voices, preferably with the main theme by the women's voices and the second theme by the men.

Each of these themes may be sung in up to four parts, and when used together, up to a total of eight parts. This sort of large combination should not be abused, but be kept for the final stages of the canon.

Credo II

Because of its simplicity, this four-part canon should be sung by all. Rhythmic evenness is helped by having a guitar play the note C on each beat. Above the canon, soloists may sing the text of the Creed on the two sustained notes that are given, *C* and *G,* with a total independence of rhythm and tempo.

On the other hand, the conclusion with its two written out *Amen's* should be made to correspond exactly to the response formula which stops on a final "credo" in C major.

Jubilate Deo

The seventeenth century composer Praetorius wrote the theme of this canon. Jacques Berthier has provided a choral accompaniment and instrumental countermelodies.

Pater sancte

Litany version: with verses in English sung over the softly rendered two-part canon.

Meditative version: performed in the same way as the *ostinato* responses in two-part canon with instrumental counter-melodies sounding above (refer to the Instrumental Edition).

Per crucem

Simple meditative version: for two voices only, in which a phrase in chorale style (Ⓐ Ⓒ Ⓔ) is always paired with an ornate phrase (Ⓑ Ⓓ Ⓕ) resulting in the following sequence: Ⓐ, then Ⓑ Ⓐ, then Ⓒ Ⓑ, Ⓓ Ⓒ, etc.

The full version is in six voices.

Sanctus

The cantor can sing the full liturgical text in English or Latin above the canon.

Tibi Deo

The *chorale* is sung by all, either in unison or in canon Ⓐ Ⓑ — Ⓒ Ⓓ and the two-part *canon* by cantors or choral group.

AGNUS DEI

Lamb of God, you take away the sins of the world, have mercy on us; grant us peace.

Canon

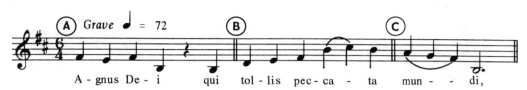

A - gnus De - i qui tol - lis pec - ca - ta mun - - di,

(To conclude, some sopranos and tenors of
the choir may sing the following several
times as an ostinato.)

Mi - se - re - re no - bis.
(Do - na no - bis pa - cem).

Do - na no - bis pa - cem.

Accompaniments

Keyboard

Guitar

Choir

(hum)

ALLELUIA

Canon

Accompaniments

Keyboard

Guitar

BENEDICITE DOMINO
Bless the Lord, all you works of the Lord.

BENEDICTUS

Blessed is he who comes in the name of the Lord.

Principal Canon

Be - ne -di -ctus qui ve - nit, Be - ne - di -ctus qui ve - nit, in

no - mi - ne, in no - mi - ne, in no - mi - ne Do - mi - ni.

Secondary Canon

Soprano or Instrument (Oboe or Trumpet)

Be - ne -di -ctus qui ve - nit, Be - ne - di -ctus qui ve - nit,

Be - ne - di -ctus qui ve - nit, in no - mi - ne Do - mi - ni.

Accompaniments

Keyboard or Instruments

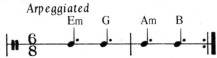

Guitar

Arpeggiated

Em   G   Am   B

Choir or Instruments

CANTATE DOMINO

(Four canons and one chorale on the same harmonic pattern using the same accompaniments)

1. Cantate Domino

Sing to the Lord, rejoice in God.

♩ = 100

Can - ta - te Do - mi - no. Al - le - lu -ia, al - le - lu - ia!

Ju - bi - la - te De - o.

2. Glory to the Father

Glo - ry to the Fa - ther al - might - y, glo - ry to his

Son, Je - sus Christ, glo - ry to the Spir -it of life, now and for ev - er. A - men.

3. Gloria II (for Christmas)

Glory to God in the highest, and peace to his people on earth.

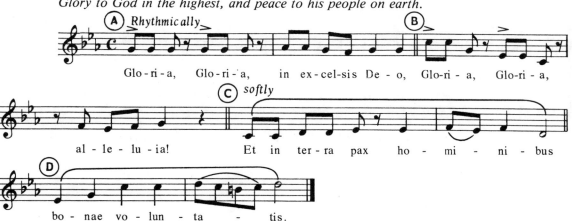

Rhythmically

Glo - ri - a, Glo - ri - a, in ex - cel - sis De - o, Glo - ri - a, Glo - ri - a,

softly

al - le - lu - ia! Et in ter - ra pax ho - mi - ni - bus

bo - nae vo - lun - ta - tis.

4. Veni Creator Spiritus (for Pentecost)

Come, Holy Spirit

Accompaniments

Keyboard

Guitar

Choir

N.B.: The Easter chorale "Surrexit Dominus" (p. 26) is sung with these same accompaniments.

CHRISTUS VINCIT — JUBILATE COELI

Christ conquers, Christ reigns, Christ rules.
Heaven and earth rejoice for Jesus Christ is truly risen.

Double Canon (2nd canon ad lib.)

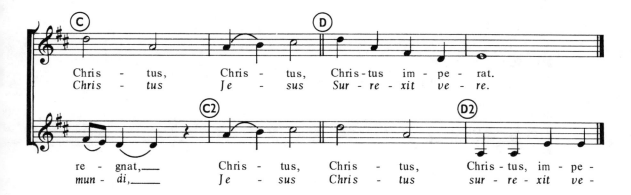

Coda

(As each voice of the canon concludes, go to one or more of the following 5 segments. Various combinations are possible.)

The piece ends on the first measure (D major chord) with the word Amen

92

Accompaniments

Keyboard

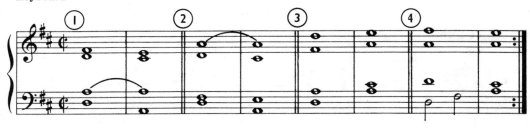

Guitar

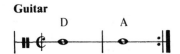

Choir

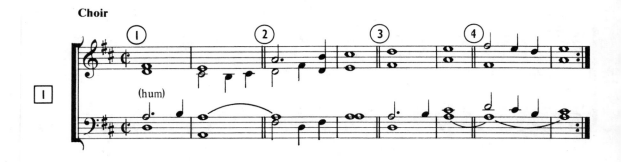

CREDO II

We believe in one God, one Lord and one Spirit.

Ostinato Response (in Canon)

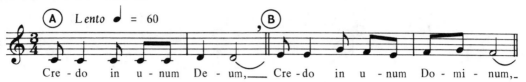

Cre - do in u - num De - um,__ Cre - do in u - num Do - mi - num,__ Cre - do in u - num De - um,__ Cre - do in u - num Spi - ri - tum.__

Verses

(The Nicene or Apostles Creed is freely chanted)

A - - men, a - - men!

To Finish:

Credo in unum

Credo!

Accompaniments

Keyboard

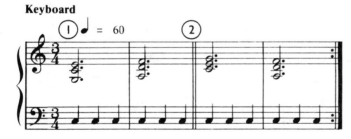

Guitar, Bass, Cello or Low Percussion

(on the note C)

94

DA PACEM DOMINE

Give peace, O Lord.

Ostinato (All)

Da pa - cem Do - mi - ne, Da

Canon (Choir - 3 voices)

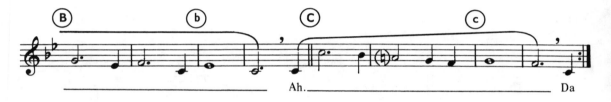

Da pa - cem Do - mi - ne, Da pa - cem Do - mi - ne, Ah.__

Ah._____ Da

Accompaniments

Keyboard or Instruments

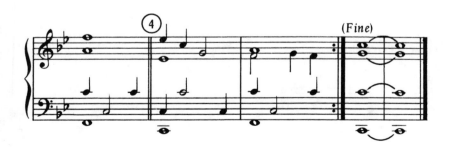

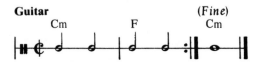

Guitar

Cm   F   (*Fine*)
                      Cm

Choir

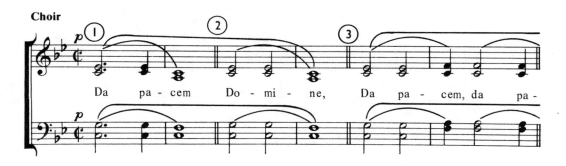

Da pa - cem Do - mi - ne, Da pa - cem, da pa -

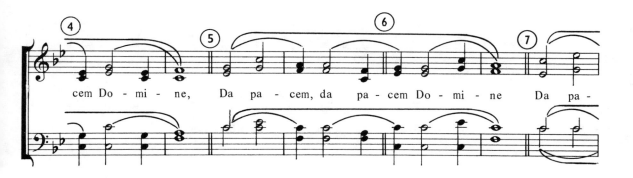

cem Do - mi - ne, Da pa - cem, da pa - cem Do - mi - ne Da pa -

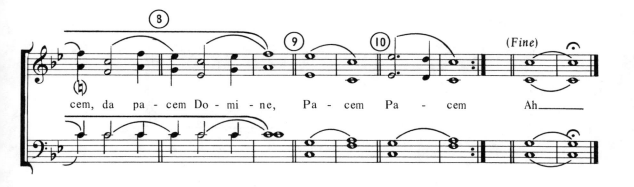

cem, da pa - cem Do - mi - ne, Pa - cem Pa - cem Ah _____

FOR YOURS IS THE KINGDOM

Canon

A ♩ = 96 *Largo*

For yours is the King-dom, for yours is the power

B for yours is the King-dom, for yours is the power

C for yours is the glo-ry, for ev-er, A - men!

D for yours is the glo-ry, for ev-er, A - men!

Accompaniments

Keyboard

Guitar

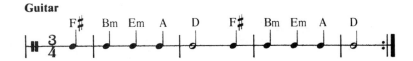

F♯ Bm Em A D F♯ Bm Em A D

GLORIA III

Glory to God in the highest. Alleluia!
Christ is born today, the Savior has appeared.

Principal Canon

Glo - ri - a, glo - ri - a, in ex - cel - sis De - o!

Glo - ri - a, glo - ri - a, al - le - lu - ia, al - le - lu - ia!

Secondary Canon - for Cantors or Choir (Unison, or in 2 Voice Canon at Ⓐ and Ⓑ).

1. Soprano, Tenor

Ho - di - e Chri - stus na - tus est, Sal - va - tor ap - pa - ru - it.

Al - le - lu - ia, al - le - lu - ia. (-ia). Glo - ri - a, glo - ri -

a, in ex - cel - sis De - o. Glo - ri - a, glo - ri - a, al - le - lu - ia.

2. Alto, Bass (Variation in small notes)

Ho - di - e Chri - stus na - tus est, Sal - va - tor ap - pa - ru - it.

Ho - di - e Chri - stus na - tus est, Sal - va - tor ap - pa - ru - it.

(-it) Glo - ri - a, glo - ri - a, in ex - cel - sis De -
(-ia)

o. Glo - ri - a, glo - ri - a, al - le - lu - ia.

98

Keyboard or Instruments

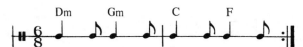

Guitar

Rhythms may be added by small percussion instruments.

Choir

(hum)

HOSANNA

Hosanna in the highest.

Canon

Ho - san - na, ho - san - na, ho - san - na in ex - cel - sis. Ho -

Accompaniments

Keyboard

Guitar

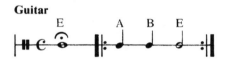

Choir

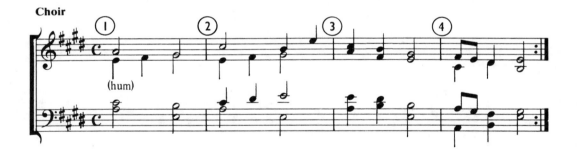

(hum)

Soprano or Instrument (at the end of the Canon)

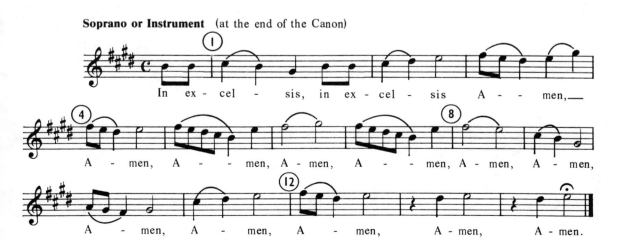

In ex - cel - sis, in ex - cel - sis A - men,____

A - men, A - men, A - men, A - men, A - men, A - men,

A - men, A - men, A - men, A - men, A - men.

JUBILATE DEO

Rejoice in God.

Canon (Praetorius)

Ju - bi - la - te De - o, Ju - bi - la - te De - o, A - le - lu - ia.

Accompaniments (Jacques Berthier)

Keyboard

(Fine)

Guitar

C F G

Choir

Ju - bi - la - te De - o,

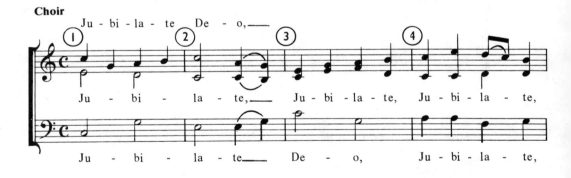

Ju - bi - la - te,___ Ju - bi - la - te, Ju - bi - la - te,

Ju - bi - la - te___ De - o, Ju - bi - la - te,

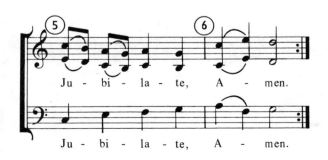

Ju - bi - la - te, A - men.

Ju - bi - la - te, A - men.

JUBILATE, SERVITE

Rejoice in God all the earth. Serve the Lord with gladness.

Canon - (2 Voices)

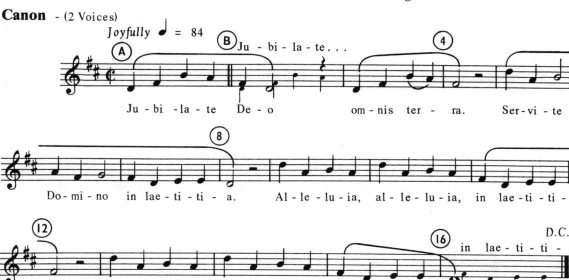

Ju - bi - la - te De - o om - nis ter - ra. Ser - vi - te

Do - mi - no in lae - ti - ti - a. Al - le - lu - ia, al - le - lu - ia, in lae - ti - ti -

a. Al - le - lu - ia, al - le - lu - ia, in lae - ti - ti - a!

Accompaniments

Keyboard or Instruments

(Fine)

Guitar

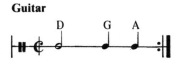

D   G   A

102

Choir

Choir (2 mixed voices)

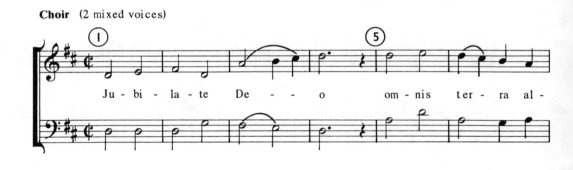

Ju - bi - la - te De - - o om - nis ter - ra al -

le - lu - ia, Ser - vi - te Do - mi - no in lae - ti - ti - a.

LAUDAMUS TE

We praise you, Lord.

Canon

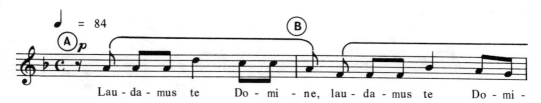

Accompaniments

Keyboard or Instruments

Guitar

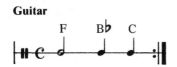

Choir

MAGNIFICAT

My soul magnifies the Lord.

Principal Canon

Ma - gni - fi - cat, Ma - gni - fi - cat, Ma - gni - fi - cat a - ni - ma

me - a Do - mi - num. Ma - gni - fi - cat, Ma - gni - fi - cat, Ma-gni - fi - cat a - ni - ma me - a!

Secondary Canon (or unison choir with trumpet)

Ma - gni - fi - cat, Ma - gni - fi - cat, a - ni - ma me - a

Do - mi - num, a - ni - ma me - a Do - mi - num.

Accompaniments

Keyboard

Guitar

G   C   D7   G

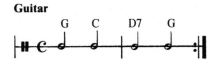

OSTENDE NOBIS

Lord, show us your mercy. Amen! Come soon!

Principal Canon

Accompaniments

Keyboard

Guitar

A   Dm   Gm   A   A

Choral Accompaniment I

A – men!   A – men!   A – men!

A – men!   A – men!   A – men!

Secondary Canon (or Choral Accompaniment II) Basses and Altos

Os – ten – de no – bis Do – mi – ne, mi – se – ri – cor – di – am tu – am Os –

Choral Accompaniment III

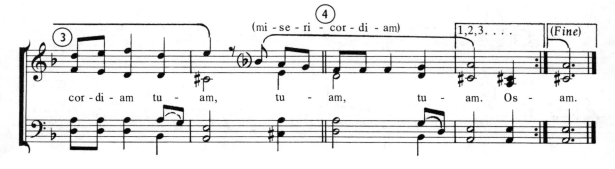

Os – ten – de – no – bis, no – bis Do – mi – ne, mi – se – ri –

(mi – se – ri – cor – di – am)

cor – di – am tu – am,   tu – am,   tu – am. Os – am.

PATER SANCTE

Holy Father, listen to our pleading.

Canon

Pa - ter san - cte, Pa - ter san - cte, ex -

au - di de - pre - ca - ti - o - nem no - stram.

Accompaniments

Guitar

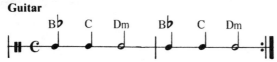

Choir

(hum)

108

Soprano (ad lib.)

Ⓐ Pa - ter san - cte, Pa - ter san - cte, ex -

Ⓑ au - di de - pre - ca - ti - o - nem no - stram.

Verses (litany)

Cantor   2nd Cantor
                                                              or Sopranos

Ⓐ 1. Gra - cious Lord, hear the prayer of your peo - ple. (Ex -

Ⓑ au - di de - pre - ca - ti - o - nem no-stram.) Ⓐ 2. Look on us with your Fa - ther - ly love. Ex -

Ⓑ Ⓐ au - di. . . . 3. Store up in us, the fire____ of your Spir - it. Ⓑ

Ⓐ 4. Help us live our lives as a peo - ple rec - on - ciled. Ⓑ Ⓐ 5. Be the de - fend - er of

Ⓑ Ⓐ those who are op - pressed. 6. Pro - tect us from e - vil, par - don our of - fen - ses. Ⓑ

Ⓐ 7. Give to our hearts the fer - or of faith, give to our hearts the fer - or of love. Ⓑ

Ⓐ 8. A - men. Ⓑ A - men. A - men. A - men.

* Choose either part.

PER CRUCEM

By your cross and passion, and by your holy resurrection, deliver us, O Lord.

Canon

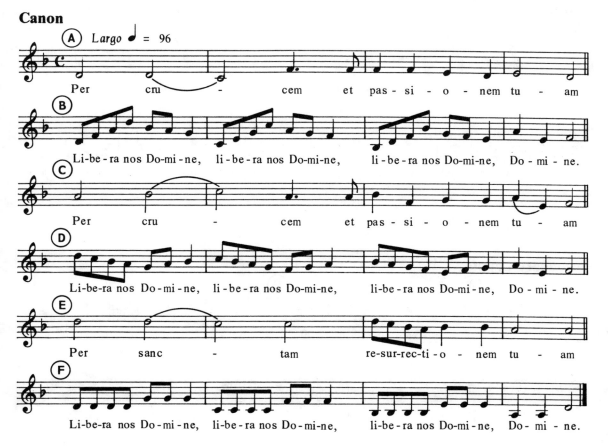

A Largo ♩ = 96

Per cru - cem et pas-si-o-nem tu - am

B
Li-be-ra nos Do-mi-ne, li-be-ra nos Do-mi-ne, li-be-ra nos Do-mi-ne, Do-mi-ne.

C
Per cru - cem et pas-si-o-nem tu - am

D
Li-be-ra nos Do-mi-ne, li-be-ra nos Do-mi-ne, li-be-ra nos Do-mi-ne, Do-mi-ne.

E
Per sanc - tam re-sur-rec-ti-o - nem tu - am

F
Li-be-ra nos Do-mi-ne, li-be-ra nos Do-mi-ne, li-be-ra nos Do-mi-ne, Do-mi-ne.

Accompaniments

Keyboard

Guitar

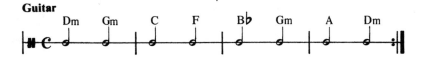

Dm Gm C F B♭ Gm A Dm

SALVATOR MUNDI

Savior of the world, save us, free us.

Principal Canon

Secondary Canon

Accompaniments

Keyboard

Guitar

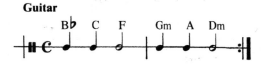

Choir

Verse

(To be sung after the principle theme is sung in unison, and before singing it in canon.)

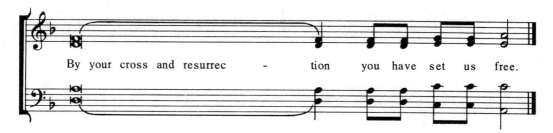

By your cross and resurrec - tion you have set us free.

Choir (With the canon)

(hum)

SANCTUS
Holy Lord, God of hosts.

Canon

Sanctus, Sanctus, Sanctus Dominus Deus Sabaoth, Deus Sabaoth.

Verses

Cantor
English

Holy, holy, holy Lord, God of pow'r and might. Heaven and earth are full of your glory. Hosanna in the highest. Blest is he who comes in the name of the Lord. Hosanna in the highest.

Latin

Pleni sunt coeli et terra gloria tua. Hosanna in excelsis. Benedictus qui venit in nomine Domini Hosanna in excelsis.

* Choose either part.

Accompaniments

Keyboard

Guitar

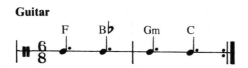

Choir

SURREXIT DOMINUS VERE II

The Lord is truly risen! Christ is risen today!

Canon

Accompaniments

TIBI DEO

To you, God the Father, through the Son and in the Holy Spirit,
be all honor and glory for ever and ever. Amen.

Canon

Ti - bi De - o Pa - tri, per Fi - li - um, in Spi - ri - tu

om - nis ho - nor et glo - ri - a, per sae - cu - la. A - men!

Chorale (unison)

Ti - bi De - o glo - ri - a. Glo - ri - a, glo - ri - a!

Al - le - lu - ia, glo - ri - a! Al - le - lu - ia, glo - ri - a!

Accompaniments

Keyboard

Guitar

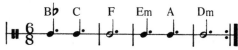

Choir

LITURGICAL AND THEMATIC INDEX

I. Biblical and Liturgical Texts in English

II. Prayers of Intercession — Litanies in English

III. Songs for Meditation

118

IV. **Songs of Praise**

See also the Psalms (I) for the response to a reading, and the
Songs of Meditation (III) and Praise (IV) for communion or
thanksgiving after communion.

VI. The Liturgical Year

INDEX